The Trident Attack for
Winning Basketball

THE TRIDENT ATTACK FOR WINNING BASKETBALL

by

Stephen L. Stephens

and

Richard Versace

Parker Publishing Company, Inc.
West Nyack, N.Y.

*The Trident Attack for Winning
Basketball*

*by Stephen L. Stephens
and
Richard Versace*

© 1969 BY

Parker Publishing Company, Inc.
West Nyack, N.Y.

Library of Congress
Catalog Card Number: 77-75385

PRINTED IN THE UNITED STATES OF AMERICA
13-930941-1 BC

DEDICATION

To Connie, Jill, Honor, David, and Julie; without whose understanding this book could not have been written.

ACKNOWLEDGMENTS

We would like to take this opportunity to thank one of the most knowledgeable basketball men in the history of the game, Coach Harold E. (Bud) Foster, former Head Basketball Coach at The University of Wisconsin. It is mainly due to his training and ideas that many of the following patterns appear in this book.

We would also like to thank Marshall Simonsen, who provided the photographs for the photo series sections in the book.

FOREWORD

Every basketball coach must teach the fundamentals, keep things simple, and then have the team go out and do what it does best, always taking advantage of the players' individual skills. Steve Stephens and Richard Versace incorporate these basic winning principles into one controlled package—the Trident Offense.

The program in this book is simple enough so that high school talent can readily grasp it, yet intricate enough to be effective against the modern variations of the man-to-man and zone defenses used today.

The Trident Offense system attacks problems involved in all aspects of the game and has solutions for everyone involved. Every coach should read this book because every coach will learn from it.

—Ed Macauley
Former All-Pro Center
Saint Louis Hawks

KEY FEATURES OF THE TRIDENT ATTACK

This book explains what we believe is the finest offensive attack available, the Trident Offense, which has been our equalizer against stronger opponents and which has won games against opponents of equal ability.

We have taken the name Trident from a mythological reference. King Neptune's three-pronged spear was called a trident. Just as the spear was three-pronged, our man-for-man attack has three basic patterns. The basic patterns are the Direct Pass Pattern, the Bounce Pass Pattern, and the Special Split. Our zone attack also has three basic patterns: Regular, Overloaded Diamond, and Attacking the Notch.

Also, each pattern incorporates three distinct options. Thus, each of the Trident's patterns contains a Trident option.

In the game of basketball, a team can win if it has better material than the other team. It can fast break, it can free-lance, it can do almost anything it wants to and still win. When the team you play is as good as you or better, then the game becomes really challenging. Now, your methods of attack, your defense, your organization, and your preparation play an increasingly important role. The difference between the winner and the loser of an evenly matched game can depend upon how much your offense helps the individual's prowess. The Trident Offense, used against man-for-man defenses, has enabled us to defeat man-for-man opponents consistently. It has so helped our players that they desperately want opponents to use a man-for-man defense. Our zone attack has been equally successful, and our players have come to believe that they can defeat any team that plays man-for-man or zone regardless of the opponents' individual abilities.

I first came in contact with the Trident Offense after I had met Coach Stephens and our conversation turned to my need of a more effective offense. His answer was what I consider to be the core of the Trident's success. He said that of all the things he had ever done in basketball, nothing had satisfied him, and he wanted something that was "darn tough" every time he came down the floor. The Trident Offense is "darn tough" every time you come down the floor.

I was convinced of the need for something I could have confidence in, and the Trident Offense seemed to be the answer. The following experiment took place: Coach Stephens agreed to teach me the Trident Offense in private skull sessions during the summer, and I would use the basic Trident Offense with my basketball team, adding any variations I wanted. The results were rewarding, and I was lucky because I could call Coach Stephens if I had a problem. In our presentation of the Trident Offense we shall keep in mind that you, the reader, will want to use the Trident Offense and that it is up to us to help you implement this offense with your team.

Hopefully, Coach Stephens' presentation of the Trident Offense itself and my insights into some of the actual problems that arise in teaching on the high school level will aid the reader in his development of an offense that is indeed "darn tough" every time it comes down the floor.

RICHARD VERSACE

Contents

1

Power Factors in the Trident Strategy

The Trident philosophy has several general principles—(1) in order to win you must be disciplined, (2) you must be able to control the game, (3) there must be balanced scoring and every player must be a threat to score, (4) as regards the fast break—look for it and take advantage of the break when you have the defense outnumbered, and (5) the offense must be able to handle all types of defenses and be adaptable to the talent available. The reason we feel the offense must be disciplined is that turnovers will be reduced, fouls will be kept at a minimum, and the offense will provide shots for the player who can't score on his own.

The offense must also have the ability to obtain quick shots and the versatility to slow down a superior fast-break team. The effectiveness of the offense should not be reduced because a team is not deep in bench strength. This offense can be 100 per cent effective with six to eight players. The offense that requires frequent substitutions will result in unnecessary losses. The team that will win is the team that is flexible and adapts to situations as they arise. It is our belief that the Trident Offense is capable of being disciplined, but it is also flexible—flexible in terms of the speed at which it may be run and in terms of the number of shots that may be taken.

From the general statement of our philosophy we derive five specific principles upon which the Trident Offense is built. In reading these principles it should be noted that in all of the premises there is an attempt to organize various phases of offensive basketball. "Organization is the key to success."

The key to our Trident philosophy of basketball is to organize the rebounding so that we are *always* in position for the second shot. This is the primary premise upon which the offense is built. It is our firm belief that offensive rebounding, to be effective, *cannot* be left to chance or, as some coaches say, to those who really want the ball. We stress the rebounding triangle, but place even more emphasis on getting the "back door" rebounding position. As a result, the offense is designed to have a strong rebounder in this position at all times.

Our second consideration, and next in importance, is the principle of "going for the lay-in." Obviously, all the shots will not be of the lay-in variety, but we feel the pressure applied to the defense will cause it to sag to the point where we are then left a medium to short jumper. Also, if the lay-in threat is not there, we become vulnerable to the pressure defenses so popular today.

Our third consideration is to have an offense that will free shooters in areas where our boys were most accurate. This lends itself to the development of drills, particularly "spot shooting" drills, where field goal percentages can be greatly improved (see Chapter 11). Therefore, the shots that the offense gives us are the shots that we practice.

Our fourth consideration is the belief that the ball must be moved quickly and accurately. As with many coaches we have often admonished our players to "move the ball faster," but have never told them where to move it. Therefore, in designing the offense, we organized our ball movement.

Our last consideration is player movement without the ball. Here we try to encourage the individual players to put as much of their own personalities into their faking and the controlling of their defensive men as possible. Moving without the ball is most important in timing, freeing the player for the score, and occupying the players who would otherwise be aiding their teammates on defense.

These, then, are the basic principles upon which the Trident Attack is built. But more specifically, the organization of the rebounding is the single principle that makes this offense a powerful and effective attack.

2

Player Alignment and Homework
in the Trident Attack

KEY FOR DIAGRAMS

The following symbols will be used in explaining our diagrams:

①	Left guard
②	Right guard
③	Left forward
④	Right forward
⑤	Center
⟶	Path of the player
----➤	Path of the ball
∿➤	Dribbler
⟳	Man with the ball
✕	Defensive man

FLOOR ALIGNMENT

When guards 1 and 2 move into the attacking court or front court we indicate the ideal positions to be 3 to 5 feet outside of the foul lane extended (Diagram 2-1). This gives the guard controlling the ball a position from which he may make any pass and have a proper angle. The guard without the ball will be approximately the same distance outside of the foul lane but should also be a step nearer to the ten-second line. This enables him to receive a pass from his partner guard with a greater degree of safety. From these positions both men can quickly initiate any part of the Trident Offense.

The forwards, 3 and 4, adjust their floor alignment with respect to the ball. The forward 3, on the same side of the

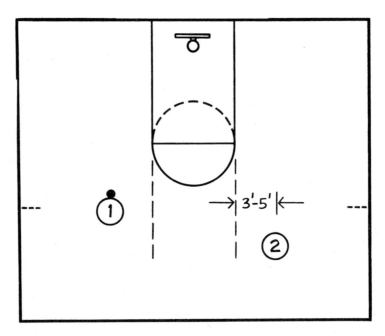

Diagram 2-1

floor as the ball, moves to a position midway between the sideline and the foul lane. He will also approximate a position equidistant from the base line and the foul line extended (Diagram 2-2). We tell our players that they may not always be able to get to this position due to the defense or the position of the passing guard, but that this is the ideal for which they should be striving.

The forward away from the ball, 4, moves to a position approximately 3 feet (one step) outside the foul lane. He should work one to two steps deeper toward the base line. From this position he is able to move quickly to the "back door" rebound area if a shot is taken, and he may readily initiate his responsibilities to the offense. By "back door" rebound area we mean the inside position on the side of the basket opposite the side from which the shot is taken.

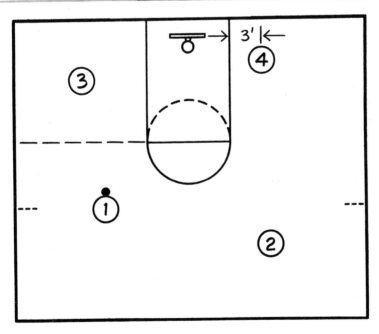

Diagram 2-2

Our center, 5, takes a position just above the foul line with his back to the basket (Diagram 2-3). He stands approximately in the middle of the foul circle. From this position he should be able to sense or feel the position of his defensive man, in addition to being alert for the ball and the positions of 1 and 2's defensive men. He should have a hand up to indicate a target to 1 and be ready to meet the pass that may be thrown to him.

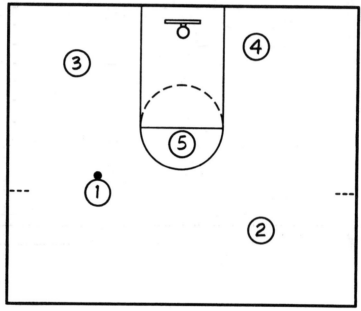

Diagram 2–3

When all of our players have obtained their ideal positions, they are now able, with proper "homework" and a quick two or three steps, to be available for the ball and to be in a passing lane with a safe angle to the ball (Diagram 2-4).

THE THEORY OF HOMEWORK

Just as the student in the classroom is given assignments

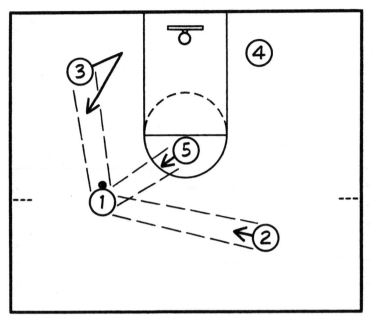

Diagram 2–4

that he must fulfill for success in school, so must the basketball player without the basketball fulfill certain assignments for his team's success. We try to give all five players things to do without the ball; however, there are many times when the player must express himself individually to get free to receive a pass. These things that a player does on his own to free himself—we call *homework*. The command "Do your homework!" has an effect all its own and points out to the player his responsibility for freeing himself.

Presented here are two of the homework maneuvers that seem to work well for our players.

 The Walk

Of all the possible maneuvers involved in "doing your homework," our players seem to find the walk most effective. The offensive player nonchalantly walks into his defensive

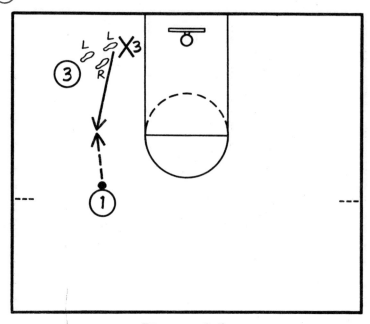

Diagram 2-5

man, being very careful not to put his hands on the defensive player. There will be an instant (as the two bodies touch) when both will be perfectly still. It is then that the offensive player pushes away with the foot opposite the direction in which he intends to go and breaks directly for the ball (Diagram 2-5). We feel this is effective because it includes both change of direction plus change of speed.

The Church Step

So named because it keeps the defensive player "honest," the church step is a maneuver which depends more on change of direction than on change of speed. The offensive player convincingly and quickly starts in one direction, plants his foot, and breaks in the opposite direction, usually toward the ball (Diagram 2-6).

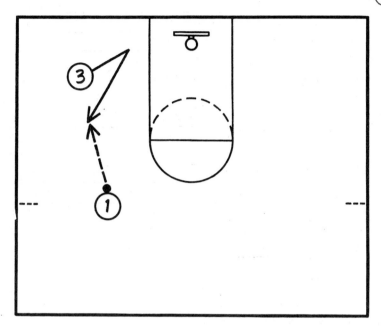

Diagram 2–6

PLAYER CHARACTERISTICS

One of the reasons, we feel, it is important to number our players is that it keeps us thinking about the characteristics of the players in those positions. The following characteristics will be given with the ideal player in mind. It is true, however, that players with other abilities may be just as effective in their own way.

The guards, 1 and 2, can be interchanged and can, of course, play either guard position. Generally we make no distinction as to right or left guard; however, in our thinking, 1 is usually the best ball handler, passer, and playmaker. We like to have him be the "take charge" player on our club. He should be an excellent dribbler and capable of scoring effectively from within 20 feet. The other guard, 2, should be bigger and probably a better shooter. He should be capable of scoring from medium to long range. He should also be the better rebounder and be an effective scorer from in close. We also like to have both 1 and 2 be adept at driving hook shots and to spend considerable time developing this shot.

The forwards, for any offense, should ideally be big, strong men who are capable rebounders and scorers. But, as you know, pairs of forwards like these do not always come along just when you need them. In spite of this, the Trident Offense can be effective with one forward, usually #3 for us, being a smaller, more mobile man. He should then be a fine scorer with a strong jump shot and above-average driving ability. On the other hand, 4 can be a bigger, stronger, less mobile man. He will be effective if he is an above-average rebounder and has a jump shot and good touch from within 15 feet. Both forwards must be fine passers and be capable of good judgment.

The Trident Offense is built around #5. He need not be an extremely good outside shooter, but he must be an outstanding jumper and rebounder. He is the man most often placed in the prime rebounding area, the back door. As a result of this offense, 5 will usually be either your leading scorer or your highest percentage shooter.

HELPFUL HINT IN TEACHING THE TRIDENT

1. Forwards should strive for ideal position when receiving the ball. Failure to do this forces the offensive man beyond scoring range.

3

The First Feature: Direct Pass Pattern— Man-For-Man Attack

The direct pass pattern is the heart of the Trident Offense. It has proved itself to be so effective that on occasion it has been the only offensive pattern necessary to defeat a man-for-man opponent. This past year, for example, one opposing coach found it necessary to change to a zone defense for the first time in his career.

Since we consider this direct pass pattern the most vital portion of the man-for-man offense we would like to discuss it first. This pattern was designed to include three of the most effective man-for-man maneuvers in basketball today. It includes give-and-go which is the heart of East Coast basketball; the rub-off, an extremely sound tactic borrowed from the shuffle; and the screen-away which is included in most fundamental man-for-man attacks. The Trident Offense, as a whole, actually includes almost all of the sound man-for-man maneuvers used in basketball. The direct pass pattern cleverly incorporates three of these tactics.

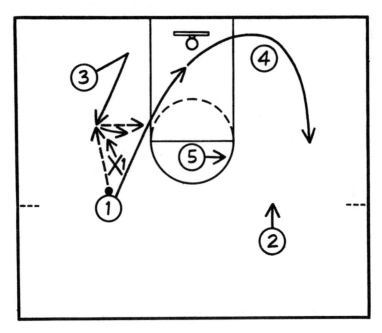

Diagram 3-1

FIRST CUTTER

The pattern is keyed by a direct pass to the forward (direct pass means any pass other than a bounce pass). In this case (Diagram 3-1), 1 passes to 3 who has done his homework and is free to receive the ball. At this point, 1 executes a give-and-go maneuver either by cutting in front of X1 or behind X1. In either case, a direct pass indicates the guard must cut inside the forward. The path of this cut depends upon the position X1 takes when the ball is passed to 3. If X1 attempts to deflect the pass or to follow the path of the ball, possibly to initiate a double team situation on 3, 1 cuts behind X1 looking for the return pass from 3.

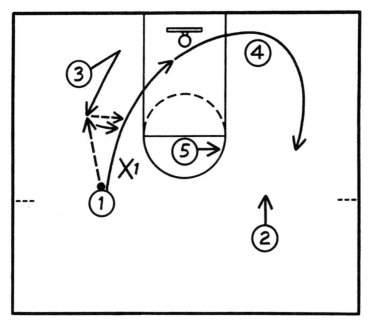

Diagram 3–2

If, however, X1 plays a more conventional defensive position, between 1 and the basket, 1 cuts in front of X1 and looks for a quick return pass from 3 (Diagram 3-2). After completing the give-and-go maneuver and not getting the ball, 1 clears the basket area by returning to a guard position. He should attempt to get back quickly to replace 2 by going out on the side opposite the ball with defensive responsibilities in mind.

As the direct pass is made from 1 to 3, 5 moves to a position away from the ball and sets a post-screen. The screen should be set at an angle which is approximately 90 degrees to the path of X2 (Diagram 3-3).

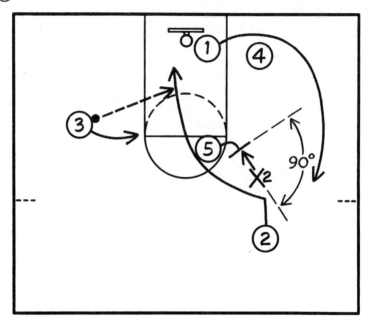

Diagram 3–3

SECOND CUTTER

As soon as the direct pass is made, 2 begins controlling his defensive man, X2, by "walking" into his man, or by a series of quick fakes. He positions X2 so that when he makes his cut to the basket X2 will be rubbed off by 5. The cut should be made so that 2's side brushes 5's side. After having looked for 1 on the give-and-go, 3 should now be ready to feed 2 as he breaks free from the rub-off. If 2 is not open, he clears the basket area by going out the opposite side and returning to replace 1's guard position.

If the second cutter, 2, detects his defensive man, X2, attempting to go behind 5, he should cut toward 3 and receive the ball approximately at the junction of the foul line and the

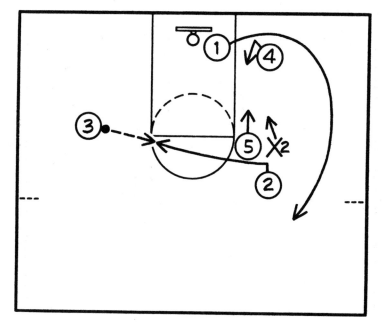

Diagram 3–4

foul circle. He should then find he is free for a jump shot. If he does not get the ball from 3 after a momentary pause, he should cut through and return to the guard position to clear the way for the third cutter (Diagram 3-4).

If 2 should find that X2 is going over-the-top and anticipating his cut; 2 should change direction and go behind 5 (Diagram 3-5). Next, 3 should look for 2 deep under the basket. If 2 does not get the ball, he clears the basket area as before.

THIRD CUTTER

After rubbing off X2, 5 drops to the back door rebounding area and secures rebounding position. As 5 drops down the back side of the foul lane, 4 cuts off from him and breaks

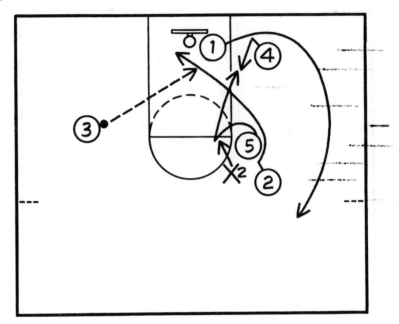

Diagram 3–5

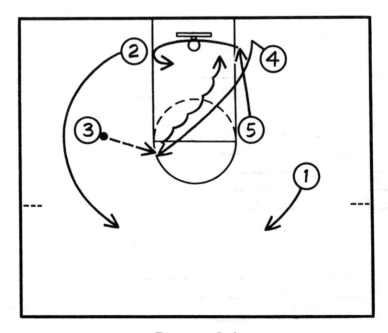

Diagram 3–6

to the ball between the foul line and the top of the key (Diagram 3-6). From this position 4 may shoot or reverse drive X4 to the basket. The center, 5, "buttonhooks" to the opposite side of the basket and again obtains back door rebound position as soon as 4 takes a dribble on his reverse drive.

Another option is available to 4 if 5 is not able to obtain rebound position. When this occurs, 5 should drift across the foul lane, keeping X5 on his back. Then 4 may pass the ball to 5 in what we call a "high-low" maneuver (Diagram 3-7). After the pass, 4 attempts to get inside position for the rebound.

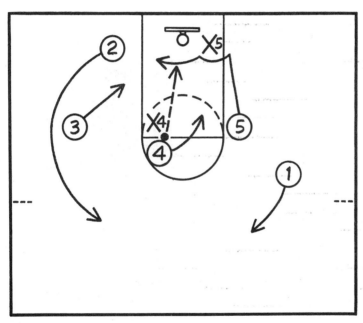

Diagram 3-7

In every instance when 3 passes to cutters 1, 2, or 4, he follows his pass expecting the ball to be returned to him or to aid in forming the rebounding triangle. It might also be noted here that 3 or any other player may drive or take a shot if a good opening presents itself. Especially, 3 may find that by faking the shot or the drive he will improve his ability to make safe, sure passes to any of the cutters.

At this point in our discussion of the Direct Pass Pattern, we would like to take a closer look at 5's position in the rub-off. Since the success of this pattern depends to such a great degree upon the maneuvers and positioning of 5, it becomes imperative that a basic level of skill and finesse be achieved in this fundamental play.

Before taking a closer look at the maneuvering and positioning of 5, we should like to mention that the Trident Offense was not designed to be a continuity offense in any way. However, after several seasons of using the Direct Pass portion of the offense, we have found the attack to be even more effective when the pattern can be run through the second and third times without waiting to set up. This continued motion aids in two important ways. First, it encourages continued ball and player movement without a pause in action, which allows a defensive team to regroup. Second, it permits a cutter to take a different path to the ball or the basket, which presents new problems to a defensive man.

In reference to the intricacies of the rub-off maneuver: the first important fundamental to be remembered is that 5 must know where 2's defensive man, X2, is playing and must set his post-screen for the rub-off on an angle. The specific angle set depends upon the path X2 takes in order to stay with 2's cut. As we stated earlier, this should be set so that 5's shoulders are at approximately 90 degrees to X2's path (Diagram 3-3).

The second fundamental to remember is that if X2 is hung up on 5's post-screen, 5 should hold his position momentarily to give 2 a good chance to break free. Then 5 pivots and drops down the foul lane to obtain the back door rebound position (Photo Series 3-1 to 3-5).

Photo 3-1. *The perfect catch. Basic starting position.*

Photo 3–2. *Offensive guard 32 fakes and walks his man toward the pivot as the offensive pivot attempts to set the 90 degree angle screen.*

Photo 3–3. *Offensive guard 32 has successfully rubbed his man off on the screen set by the offensive center. Offensive center holds his pick for two counts and pivots on his left foot to get inside rebound position.*

Photo 3–4. *Offensive guard 32 receives pass from forward and anticipates shot as defensive center 42 switches.*

Photo 3–5. *Offensive guard 32 takes short hook shot as offensive center 33 has secured the back door rebound position.*

The third fundamental to remember is that if X2 tries to avoid the rub-off by going behind 5, (Photo Series 3-6 to 3-10), 5 should immediately pivot on his left foot, catching X2 on his back, and drop to the back door rebound position. When 2 sees X2 retreat behind the center, he may want to receive the ball from 3 at the foul line for the jump shot (Photo Series 3-11 to 3-15). This is often a good maneuver since X5, the center's defensive man, usually will drop off 5 to zone the foul lane.

Photo 3–6. *Combating going behind by the defensive guard. Basic starting position.*

Photo 3–7. *The defensive guard attempts to go behind the screen.*

Photo 3-8. *The offensive center immediately pivots on his left foot and catches the defensive guard on his way to back door rebound position. Offensive guard 32 goes over the top.*

Photo 3–9. *Offensive guard 32 receives pass from forward and anticipates shot as defensive center switches.*

Photo 3–10. *Offensive guard 32 takes hook shot as offensive center 33 has secured the back door rebound position.*

Photo 3–11. *Combating waiting behind by the defensive guard. Basic starting position.*

Photo 3–12. *The defensive guard has attempted to go deep behind the screen, almost before it is set.*

Photo 3-13. *Offensive guard 32 stays high on the free throw line and receives pass as offensive center 33 has immediately pivoted on his left foot and headed down the lane. Offensive center 33 interrupts the defensive guard's path back to offensive guard 32.*

Photo 3-14. *Offensive guard 32 takes jump shot as offensive center 33 secures back door rebound position.*

Photo 3–15. *Offensive center 33 using "two hands" tips in missed shot from his back door rebound position.*

The fourth fundamental to remember is that if X2 attempts to go "over-the-top" of the post-screen set by 5, 5 should then pivot on his right foot and wait for contact from X2 before getting his back door rebound position (Photo Series 3-16 to 3-20). When this happens, 2 may want to cut behind the center and 3 should look for the second cutter, 2, under the basket.

Photo 3–16. *Combating fighting over the top by the defensive guard. Basic starting position.*

Photo 3–17. *Defensive guard attempts to fight over the screen.*

Photo 3–18. *Offensive guard 32 goes behind as offensive center 33 pivots on his right foot and momentarily catches defensive guard 12.*

Photo 3-19. *Offensive guard 32 receives pass underneath the basket and anticipates shot as defensive center 42 switches.*

Photo 3-20. *Offensive guard 32 takes short hook shot as the offensive center 33 secures the back door rebound position.*

It should be noted, too, that the Direct Pass Pattern is run to either side of the floor. For the purpose of simplicity, however, everything has been diagrammed with a pass to the left side.

HELPFUL HINTS IN TEACHING THE TRIDENT

1. *First cutter must execute the give-and-go maneuver quickly or he may congest the area being cleared for the second cutter.*

2. *The second cutter should not initiate the rub-off move too far from the post. With proper maneuvering, one or two steps should free him for the ball.*

3. *The second cutter who drifts to the junction of the foul line and the foul circle must not wait longer than two seconds to receive the ball before clearing this area for the third cutter.*

4. *The third cutter, in anticipation of the screen by 5, should walk his defensive man toward the basket to insure a successful rub-off.*

5. *The third cutter should always remember that if 5 does not have the back door rebound position he should then be open on the high-low maneuver.*

4

The Second Feature:
Bounce Pass Pattern—
Man-For-Man Attack

The Bounce Pass Pattern is used to complement the Direct Pass Pattern explained in Chapter 3. This option is used more against "sagging" or "sluffing" man-to-man defenses, although it can be effective against pressure defenses as well.

FIRST OPTION

This pattern is keyed by a bounce pass made by 1 to 3 (Diagram 4-1). Again 3 must do his homework to free himself and break to the proper passing lane. The pass made by 1 must be aimed at the outside hip of 3 to prevent his defensive man, X3, from intercepting or deflecting the ball. We also stress that 1 make the bounce pass with his outside hand, in this case his left hand, to prevent his defensive man, X1, from deflecting the ball. 1 then follows his pass going to the outside and pausing or stopping in the corner.

If, during the game, X1 attempts to double

team 3 as he goes by, 3 may then return the ball to 1 who will be free for the drive or the jump shot (Diagram 4-2).

As 1 passes to 3, 5 drops deep to the opposite side of the lane and sets a post-screen for 4, much as he did for 4 in the Direct Pass Pattern (Diagram 4-3). 4, who has controlled his defensive man, X4, rubs him off on 5 as he breaks for the basket and the ball. As 4 breaks free, 3 feeds him the ball as soon as possible since we would like 4 to attempt to score from a spot in the foul lane. (Photo Series 4-1 to 4-5).

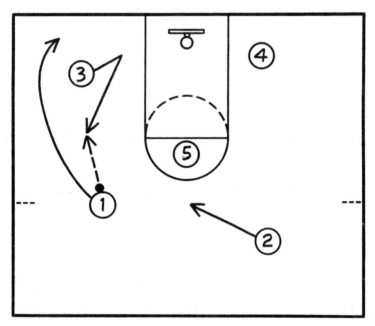

Diagram 4–1

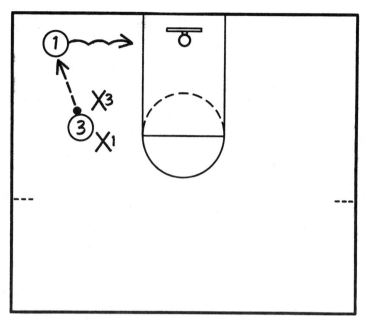

Diagram 4–2

If, on the deep post-screen, 4 detects the center's defensive man, X5, waiting for him to come over-the-top on the rub-off, he may fake this maneuver and go behind 5 (Diagram 4-4). 4 May use the same offensive maneuver should he detect his own defensive man, X4, fighting over 5's screen (Photo Series 4-6 to 4-10). Also, whenever 3 passes to 4, he should follow his pass, either for a return pass or to get rebound position. 1, who had paused in the corner, should cut along the base line whenever 3 passes to 4. If he sees the shot has already been taken, he should then go to the high rebound area near the foul line. 5, after 4 has completed the rub-off, pivots in the direction X4 has attempted to go and secures the back door rebound position. 2, meanwhile, moves to the top of the key as a safety valve and becomes available for another option.

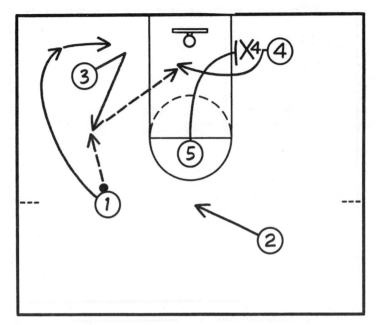

Diagram 4-3

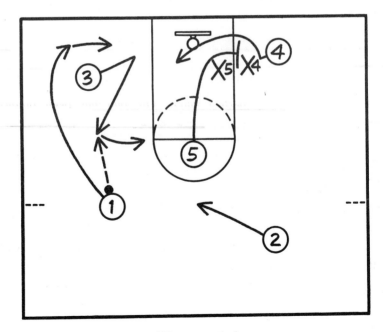

Diagram 4-4

Photo 4–1. *The perfect catch. The ball has been bounce passed to the opposite forward keying offensive center 33 to drop down to the base line. Offensive forward 32 starts walking his man toward the basket.*

Photo 4–2. *Offensive forward 32 controls his defensive man, anticipating the deep post screen.*

Photo 4–3. *Offensive forward 32 has successfully rubbed off defensive guard 12 on the offensive center 33 as the defensive center 42 starts to shift.*

Photo 4–4. *Offensive center 33 has pivoted on his left foot to catch defensive guard 12 as he attempts to fight under the screen. Offensive guard 32 receives the ball and prepares to shoot a hook shot even though defensive center 42 has shifted.*

Photo 4–5. *Offensive forward 32 takes hook shot as offensive center 33 has successfully obtained inside position on the back door rebound.*

Photo 4–6. *Combating fighting over. The ball has been bounce passed to the opposite forward, keying offensive center 33 to drop down to the base line. Offensive forward 32 starts walking his man toward the basket.*

Photo 4–7. *Offensive forward 32 attempts to control his man, but defensive forward 12 is anticipating the deep post screen.*

Photo 4–8. *Defensive forward 12 has anticipated the screen and fights over the top of it.*

Photo 4–9. *Offensive forward 32 quickly cuts under the basket to receive the ball as offensive center 33 has pivoted on his right foot to catch defensive guard 12 on his back.*

Photo 4–10. *Offensive forward 32 takes hook shot as defensive center 42 recovers. Offensive center 33 has obtained inside rebound position on the back door.*

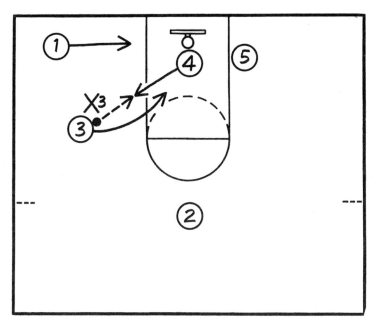

Diagram 4–5

If, when 4 rubs off, he breaks under the basket and is not open, he then cuts directly to the ball or to an open area to set a post. We tell him the ideal spot is midway between the foul line and the base line. 3 then feeds 4 and follows his pass, expecting the return handoff from 4. We emphasize to 4 that he give the ball back to 3 if he has a step on his defensive man, X3. If 3 does not get the ball, he takes the center position in the rebounding triangle. 1 also cuts along the base line, expecting the ball as 4 receives the pass from 3.

THROW-OUT OPTION

The second option open to 3, should he decide that the pass to 4 is too risky, is what we call our "throw-out" or "reverse" option. This option is keyed by the pass from 3 to 2 at

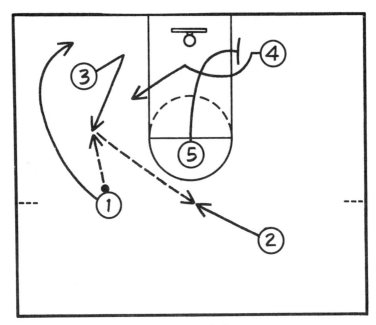

Diagram 4–6

the top of the foul circle. We tell 3 that this should be a quick chest pass, and 2 that he must come to meet the ball (Diagram 4-6).

As soon as 5 sees 2 catch the pass from 3, he breaks up the side of the foul lane to receive the ball from 2 (Diagram 4-7). 2 is told to make this a bounce pass to 5, as he is usually running hard and has a better chance of handling the ball cleanly if it comes off the floor. This bounce pass from 2 should be made with his right hand and aimed at 5's outside hip, again to prevent 5's defensive man, X5, from intercepting or deflecting the ball. As 5 receives the ball from 2, 3, who has controlled his defensive man, X3, by moving toward the basket, breaks away from 4. 5 looks to pass to 3 if he is open. We tell 5 to look for 3 as soon as he receives the ball and, if he is open, to throw a bounce pass to him. 1, meanwhile, returns to the guard position with defensive responsibility.

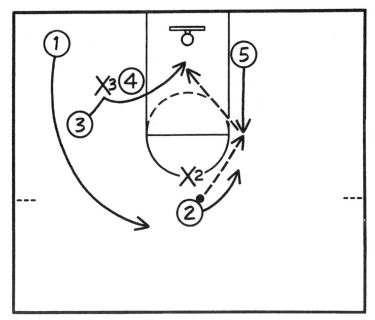

Diagram 4–7

At this point in the "throw-out" option, when 5 has received the ball from 2 and has looked, but not passed to 3, the coach may make a decision as to the completion of the option. If we feel our center, 5, is a capable driver and scorer we now give him an opportunity to beat his defensive man, X5 (Diagram 4-8). In this situation we have 5 turn toward the basket as he looks for 3 and become a threat to jump shoot if his defensive man, X5, gives him room. If X5 does challenge the jump shot we like to have 5, who is now facing the basket, cross his left foot over and drive to the board. 2, in this situation, follows his original pass to 5 but flares toward the outside expecting a release pass from 5 for the outside jumper. 4, who had set a post-screen for 3, now secures the back door rebound position. 3 also is a rebounder when he does not receive a pass from 5.

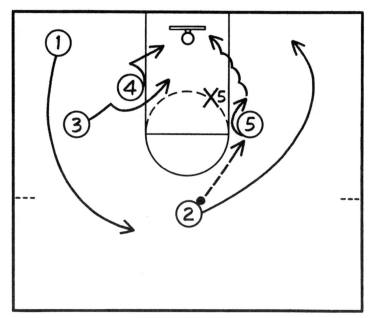

Diagram 4-8

If, however, 5 is being pressured by X5 when he receives the pass from 2, we like to have 5 reverse-drive to the basket. 2 again flares to the outside for the release pass and jump shot.

The other method a coach may use to complete the option attempts to set up 2 for the score. If 5 is not a strong enough scorer and we have good jump-shooting guards, we have 2 cut close to 5 for a handoff to 2; 5 then pivots on his left foot and rolls to the basket for the rebound position.

If when 5 pivots to hand off to 2, he notices his defensive man, X5, preparing to shift off on 2, he should then keep the ball, completing his pivot, and drive to the basket (Diagram 4-11). It is important that 5 pivot with 2's cut instead of turning in the opposite direction. The change of direction could cause him to run into X2 instead of "catching him on his back" as he goes to the basket.

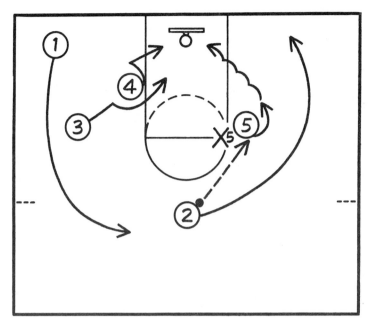

Diagram 4–9

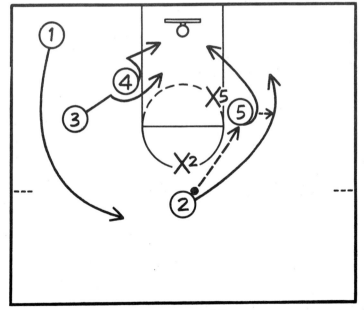

Diagram 4–10

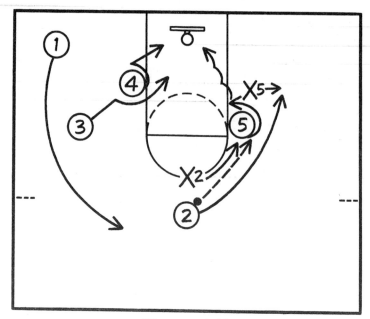

Diagram 4–11

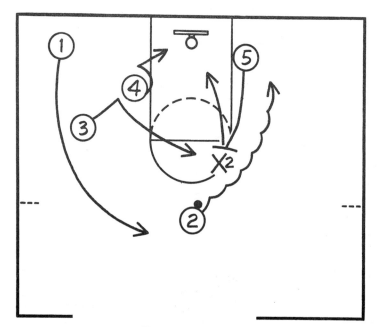

Diagram 4–12

If, during the course of the game, X2 begins to overplay the "throw-out" or "reverse" option by dropping off and preventing the pass to 5, or if X5 overplays 5 to prevent the pass, we then have 2 dribble off a rear-pick set by 5. This rear-pick variation is keyed by 2's dribble. As 2 breaks clear of the pick by 5 he may pass to 5 as he rolls to the basket, jump shoot, or pass to 3 who now comes to the high post area near the foul line.

CORNER OPTION

In the Bounce Pass Pattern, 3 has a third option available to him. We call this the "corner" option (Diagram 4-13). In this option, 3 passes to 1 in the corner. 1 now passes the ball to 4 and moves to screen 3's defensive man, X3. 3 then comes off 1's screen toward the base line looking for a pass from 4

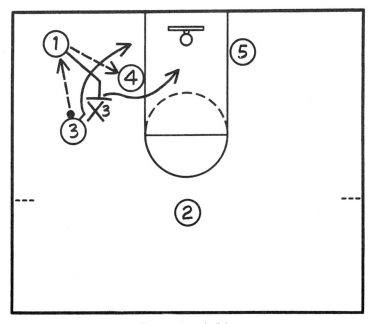

Diagram 4–13

for the drive or jump shot. 1, after screening X3, pivots on his left foot and cuts to the basket expecting a handoff from 4.

We also allow the normal scissors play on this option (Diagram 4-14). In this maneuver, 3 passes to 1 who in turn feeds the ball to 4. 1 then cuts first going over-the-top of 4, and 3 cuts to the baseline side of 4.

In these three basic options of the Bounce Pass Pattern there are enough variations to keep the opposition's defense honest. We have found that, by using the Direct Pass Pattern and the Bounce Pass Pattern to complement each other, both patterns become more effective.

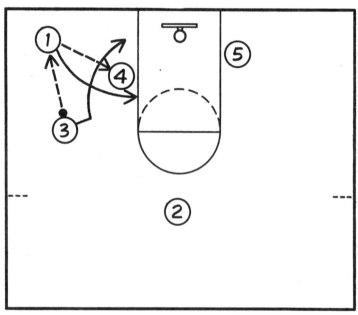

Diagram 4-14

At this point in the discussion of the Trident Offense we feel it timely to point out that we are not leaving things to chance. Look through the diagrams you have just read and you will notice that we have organized the rebounding so that we have our best rebounder in the back door position in almost every instance when a shot is taken. Most of the success we have had with the Trident Offense we attribute to the organization of the rebounding because we are not only getting good shots, but sometimes two or three good shots. This organization of the rebounding falls in line with Power Principle number one of the Trident Offense. And from a psychological viewpoint, there is no better feeling for a player to have than to know his shot, if missed, has a good chance of being tipped in.

HELPFUL HINTS IN TEACHING THE TRIDENT

1. *When teaching the Bounce Pass Pattern it is most important that the guards be made to pass the ball with their outside hand and to aim for the forward's outside hip.*

2. *When setting the deep post-screen, 5 must remember to go to a spot that will intersect the path of the forward's defensive man as he tries to stay with the forward's cut to the ball. 5 must never cut directly to the spot occupied by this defensive man to set his screen, since the defense could easily avoid it.*

3. *Remember—the rub-off by 3 in the "throw-out" option is the maneuver by which 4 is able to obtain back door rebound position.*

4. *Remember—in the "corner" option, after 1 has passed to 4, 1 must obtain a good "screening angle" on X3 by taking a quick two steps toward the basket before setting the screen on X3. Obtaining the "screening angle" must be the first move in any screening maneuver.*

5

The Third Feature:
The Pivot—
Man-For-Man Attack

In the previous chapters we have discussed the patterns of the Trident Offense which have been initiated by a pass from a guard to a forward. Because of the effectiveness of the Direct Pass and Bounce Pass Patterns it was necessary for us to build a strong attack down-the-middle. We felt this down-the-middle or pivot attack, as we think of it, should be effective enough to use every time we go down the floor.

However, it doesn't mean that when we go to the pivot attack we are deserting the outside game. The very thing that makes the pivot attack so effective is the overplaying of the Direct Pass and Bounce Pass Patterns.

As a general rule, we tell our players never to force the ball to any player or to force any pattern. If the opponents pressure the outside pass, guard-to-forward, then look to the pivot area or the other guard to attack quickly on the opposite side. Basically we have found that the better ball handler and scorer the 5 man is, the more the guards and forwards will attempt to use the pivot.

In developing our inside or pivot attack, we wanted rather simple maneuvers that could be used to get a quick basket, as well as patterns that could complement the other portions of the offense. By this we mean that if a defensive player were out of position due to overplaying a basic pattern, then we could set up a maneuver that, although different, would look somewhat the same, thus exploiting the defensive man's mistake. We also wanted patterns that would make use of the pivot from both the guard and the forward positions.

Our basic pivot attack then uses four patterns. On two of these the ball goes inside from the guard positions and on two from the forward positions.

SPECIAL SPLIT

Since we long have felt the basic scissors play to be one of the simplest yet most effective man-for-man maneuvers in basketball, it was decided that this would be the heart of our pivot attack. In most cases, when we go to our pivot attack we use our Special Split.

The first option on our Special Split is the basic scissors play. In this maneuver, 1 passes to 5, who has given him a target showing where he would like the ball. We emphasize the importance of 5's coming to meet the ball. (In most cases the teams that have difficulty running a pivot attack do so because of the poor execution of this simple fundamental.) 1 now cuts off 5, going over-the-top of his defensive man, X1. Our rule concerning this is: "The man that passes the ball to 5 always becomes the first cutter." 2 now becomes the second cutter. 2 also goes over-the-top if his defensive man "plays him

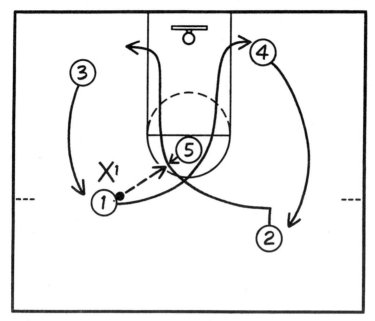

Diagram 5-1

honest." As 1 passes to 5, both 3 and 4 flare to the outside and assume the guard positions. They now have defensive responsibilities and become available for other options.

1 and 2 should always expect to get the ball from 5 when they cut off him. 1 and 2 should also expect the ball from 5 on a delayed pass after they get under the basket (Diagram 5-2). On the delayed pass, 5 should look for 1 and 2 deep, if either X1 or X2 turns his back on the ball and chases his man, then 5 may attempt the delayed pass.

If 5 does not feed 1 or 2, either on a handoff as they go by or a delayed pass under the basket, he may then shoot if he is open, or make a release pass to either 3 or 4 who have taken the guard positions for another option. When 1 and 2 realize they will not be getting the ball they turn to the outside and assume the forward positions (Diagram 5-3).

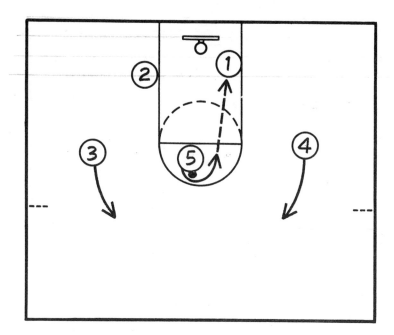

Diagram 5–2

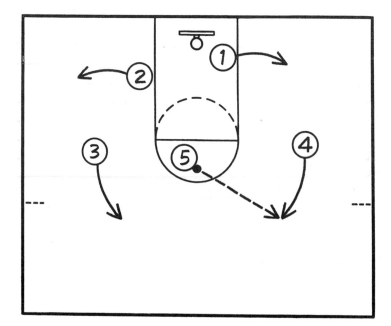

Diagram 5–3

If, when 1 passes to 5 and begins his cut over-the-top, he notices his defensive man X1 anticipating his route and overplaying his cut to the opposite side of 5, 1 may then plant his right foot and cut hard to the same side of 5 (Diagram 5-4). As 1 makes his change of direction we have him call out, "cut" to aid 5 in getting him the ball if he is open. 2 may make the same maneuver anytime his defensive man anticipates his cut over-the-top. 1 and 2 again end up on the opposite side of the floor from their original positions, and 3 and 4 flare to the guard positions.

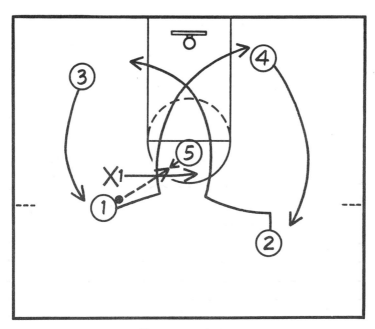

Diagram 5-4

If 2 notices that the defensive guards X1 and X2 defend this maneuver by shifting, he may cut to the same side as 1 (Diagram 5-5). This causes 5's defensive man, X5, to shift, creating a mismatch with either X1 or X2 defending against 5. Usually, however, 2 will find himself open before X5 can switch off to cover him.

If 5 should feel that a pass to either 1 or 2 is too risky and that he does not have a good shot himself, he may then throw a release pass to either 3 or 4 in the guard positions (Diagram 5-6). 4, in this case, may return the pass to 5, and with 3, scissor off 5. 1 and 2 then flare back to the guard positions. 3 and 4 have the same options available to them that the guards had the first time through. From this position the same scissors option can be run again or the guards may elect to go to the Direct Pass or Bounce Pass Patterns if they are open.

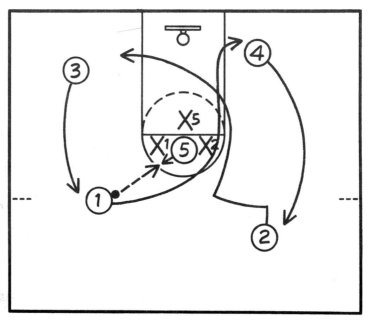

Diagram 5-5

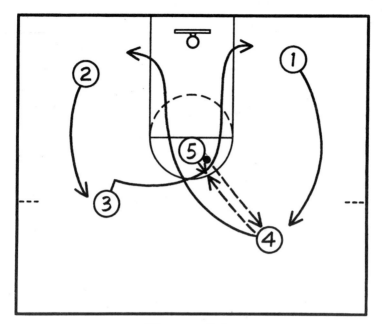

Diagram 5–6

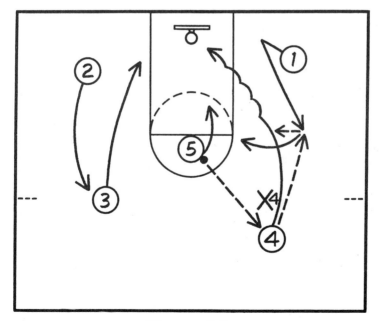

Diagram 5–7

When 5 makes a release pass to forwards 4 or 3 they have still another option available to them (Diagram 5-7). In this situation, 4 may pass to 1 and cut to the basket on a simple give-and-go maneuver. If 4 can get position on his defensive man, X4, 1 gives him the ball. 1 then follows his pass expecting the return pass for the drive or jump shot. 3, meanwhile, cuts to the basket to obtain the back door rebound position. 5 also cuts down the foul lane to be a rebounder. 2 now comes to the top of the foul circle to assume defensive responsibilities.

If, when 1 receives the pass from 4 and decides that 4 is not open on the give-and-go, he may then dribble to the guard position. This maneuver now puts the guards and forwards back in their proper positions and 1 may then decide which pattern to use (Diagram 5-8). We usually tell the forwards 3 and 4 to cut all the way to the basket on the give-and-go maneuver before returning to their normal forward positions.

We have found that the Special Split, if run properly, is the only pivot attack really necessary to keep your opponents honest on defense. It is our recommendation when a coach has a young or inexperienced team, that he limit his man-for-man arsenal to the basic patterns of the Trident Offense, namely the Direct Pass Pattern, the Bounce Pass Pattern, and the Special Split.

BLIND PIG

This particular pattern is used in an attempt to get the quick basket or to take advantage of the front line defensive men who turn and attack the high post every time the ball goes to the pivot area. The defensive front line man who does this we call the "blind pig" since he takes his eyes off his offensive man.

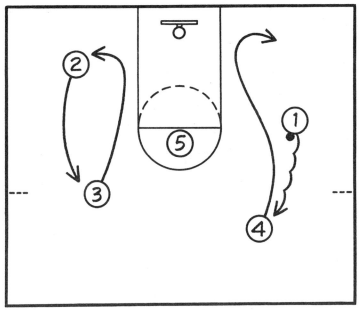

Diagram 5-8

This maneuver is usually initiated on a call from one of our offensive men as the guards move the ball into the front court. We can also make the call during a time-out when we have noticed a "blind pig" on the other team or in the closing moments of the game when we need to get a good, quick shot at the basket.

On the signal, the pattern is started with 5 moving to the same side of the foul lane as the ball and 4 breaking to an open area at the high post (Diagram 5-9). 1 usually fakes a pass to 5 or 3 to keep their defensive men honest and then passes the ball to 4 as he breaks clear at the high post position. 2 watches both the ball and his defensive man, X2, or in this case our "blind pig." 2 then cuts to the basket behind his defensive man when: (1) X2 takes his eyes off him and watches the ball as it is passed to 4 or (2) 4 touches the ball on the pass from 1. 4 then passes the ball to 2 as he breaks free on

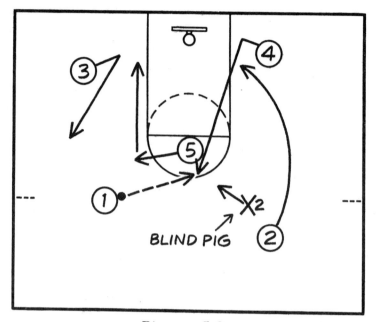

Diagram 5–9

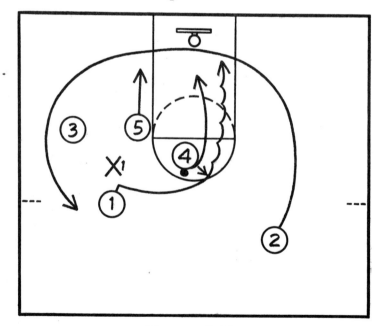

Diagram 5–10

his cut to the basket. 5 will then drop down the foul lane to obtain the back door rebound position and 4 also will drop to become a rebounder. 3 may be used either for rebounding or to aid in defensive responsibilities.

At this stage it seems fitting to point out a little trick we teach our guards, in this case 2. As 2 waits for the right time to begin his cut to the basket, he should not be working or faking his defensive man. The less 2 does to attract the attention of the "blind pig," the easier it will be for him to cut to the basket unnoticed. When the instant comes for 2 to cut, he should simply go to the basket with a slight "belly" in his cut to give 4 a better passing angle.

As 4 receives the ball from 1, he turns to look for 2 on his cut to the basket. If 2 is not open and the pass cannot be safely made, 2 should then quickly clear the basket area by returning to the guard position (Diagram 5-10). 1, after passing to 4, makes a quick break toward the basket as though executing a give-and-go maneuver. This gives 4 time to feed 2 if he is open, as well as to control his defensive man X1. 1 then plants his left foot and cuts off 4, expecting the ball for the drive or jump shot. 5 and 4 now get rebound position with 5 in the back door area. 3 then cuts to the foul line expecting a return pass from 1 for the jump shot if 1 should not have a good shot himself.

If 1 does not receive the ball as he cuts off 4, he then flares to the corner expecting a release pass for the jump shot. 4 now may attempt to beat his defensive man X4 by jump shooting or driving to the basket (Diagram 5-11). 3 again comes to the foul line area expecting a release pass for the jump shot and 5 gets the back door rebound position.

CHECK

The "check" or "double guard around" pattern as we sometimes refer to it, is the first of two patterns we use to

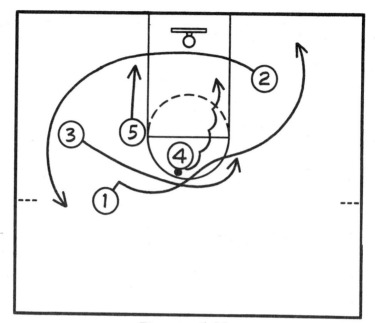

Diagram 5–11

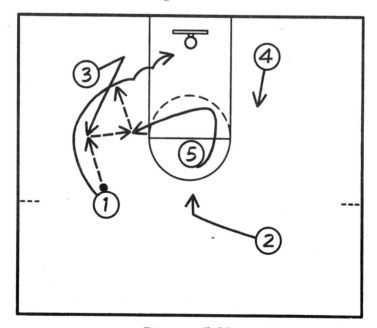

Diagram 5–12

hit the inside or pivot from the forward positions. This pattern, as you will see, is quite similar to the Bounce Pass Pattern in its initial stages but develops differently so as to exploit the defensive men who overplay the original patterns. This is also another pattern that we use in special situations or after a time-out.

The pattern is keyed by the guard with the ball, in this case 1, calling the word "check" as he moves the ball into the front court. He should make the call loudly enough and early enough to give his teammates a chance to react to the new pattern and thus eliminate confusion. 1 then passes to 3 who has done his homework, and is free to receive the ball. The pass to 3 is usually a bounce pass to give the defense the illusion of the Bounce Pass Pattern. 1 then follows his pass going outside of 3 (Diagram 5-12). 5 now moves to meet the pass as 3 throws him the ball. 5 should receive the ball at approximately the junction of the foul lane and foul line and look immediately for 1 who has continued his cut to the basket. If 1 is open or has a step on his defensive man, 5 should pass him the ball. 2 now has obtained a position above the key since he begins moving to this spot as the pass is thrown from 1 to 3 to begin the pattern. As he sees 1 receive the pass from 5 he assumes defensive responsibilities.

If, however, 1 is not open, he continues to cut beneath the basket and quickly returns to the guard position (Diagram 5-13). 3, as soon as he has passed to 5, cuts across the top half of the foul circle as though expecting a return pass from 5. 2 has now timed his cut to come tight off 3's back, expecting the handoff from 5 for the drive or jump shot. 4's job is to be available to obtain the back door rebound position. 5, after the handoff to 2, also rolls down the foul lane to be a rebounder. 3 usually drifts back to the ball side of the foul lane expecting a release pass from 2 for the jump shot. 1 now assumes the defensive responsibilities.

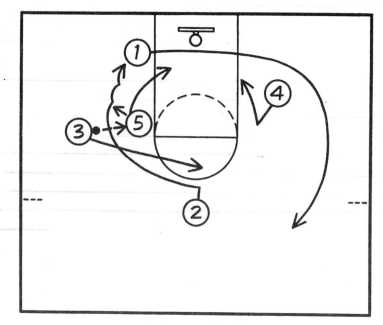

Diagram 5–13

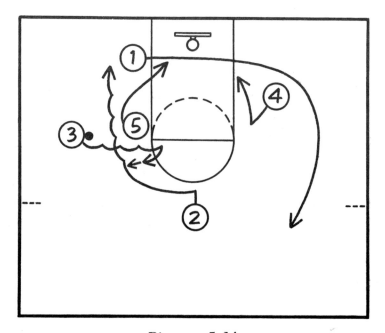

Diagram 5–14

If, after running the "check" pattern a few times, 3's defensive man, X3, drops away to discourage the pass from 3 to 5, 3 may then break on a quick dribble over-the-top of 5. 5, as he sees 3 start to dribble, should turn to face away from the basket. 3 usually should dribble about 3 feet above 5 to encourage X3, his defensive man, to go over-the-top of 5 with him (Diagram 5-14).

As 3 gets about one step beyond 5, he should stop and reverse pivot to catch X3 between himself and 5. 2, who had taken a step toward his defensive man should now cut off 3 expecting a handoff for the drive or jump shot (Diagram 5-15). 3 should then drift to the outside expecting a release pass for the jump shot and 5 should roll to obtain rebound position. 4 is again responsible for the back door rebound position and 1 for defense.

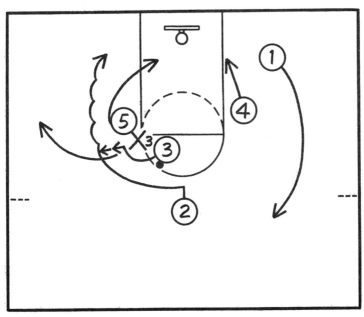

Diagram 5-15

We tell 3 that his dribble option is a good play but he should pass to 5 whenever possible since it gives us another chance to score as 1 goes under the basket as illustrated previously in Diagram 5-12.

One other possibility we give 3 on the dribble option is to continue his dribble and drive for the basket himself as he comes off 5 (Diagram 5-16). This is often quite effective if 3's defensive man, X3, waits to be able to shift and pick up 2 as he comes around. 3 may also take the jump shot from the foul line if he's open. 5 and 4 both get rebound position again and 1 has defensive responsibilities. 2 now drifts to the side of the foul lane for a release pass and jump shot should the need arise.

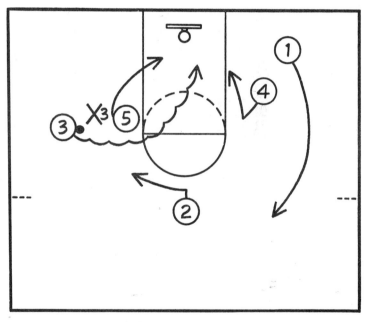

Diagram 5–16

DOUBLE CHECK

The "double check" pattern is a second pattern that complements the Bounce Pass portion of the offense. Again the ball goes to the pivot from the forward position and tends to keep the defensive center, X5, honest. This keeps X5 honest by preventing him from zoning the pivot area, as often happens in the Bounce Pass Pattern. If he zones the "double check," we bring 5 to the ball for an easy basket (Diagram 5-18).

Again the pattern is keyed by the guard who brings the ball into the front court, in this case 1. He calls "double check" giving his teammates plenty of time to react to the new pattern. We usually tell our guards to make their calls as they cross the ten-second line so that by the time they are ready for the first pass everyone will be running the same pattern. 1 now initiates the pattern by bounce passing the ball to 3's outside hip and following his pass to stop just behind 3 (Diagram 5-17). 3 then hands the ball back to 1 as 5 drops down the foul lane as if to set a post-screen for 4 in the Bounce Pass Pattern. 2 again comes to the area at the top of the key.

As 3 returns the ball to 1 he turns and cuts across the top half of the foul circle (Diagram 5-18). 5, who has faked the post-screen for 4, quickly turns and takes a low post position on the side of the foul lane. As soon as 1 passes the ball to 5 he should follow his pass, going over-the-top of 5, and expect a return handoff. We tell 5 to give 1 the ball if he has a step on his defensive man, X1. 2 now has closely cut off 3 and also 1. He also expects a handoff from 5 for the jump shot. 3 now assumes the defensive responsibilities and 4 may either help rebound or become available for a release pass at the foul line.

As a general rule, patterns such as the "blind pig," "check," and "double check" are used periodically throughout the game or in specific instances. We have on occasion, however, used

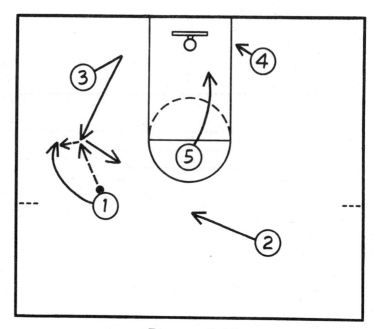

Diagram 5–17

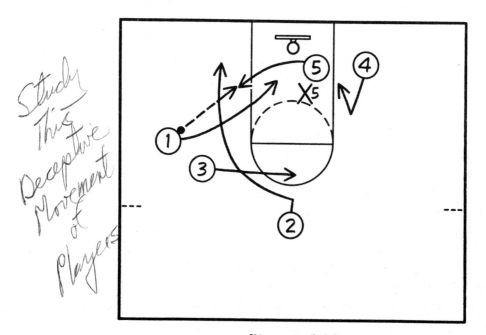

Diagram 5–18

one or more of these patterns for most of a ball game when we have found the opposition to have a great deal of trouble defensing them.

HELPFUL HINTS IN TEACHING THE TRIDENT

1. Whenever we designate a man to take a release pass position, we stress that he should be facing the basket as he receives the ball and be ready to shoot.

2. A tip to insure 5's getting open to receive the ball on the "check" pattern: have 5 start down the lane as though to screen X4 (as in the Bounce Pass Pattern) before returning to receive the ball.

3. Remember—when the guards are splitting the post they are not restricted to a scissors cut or any particular move but should make their cuts based on how their defensive men play them.

6

The Trident Outside Zone Attack

In the previous chapters we have been discussing the Trident Attack used against various types of man-for-man defenses. As we have indicated, the man-for-man patterns have been most successful and have caused many teams to change defenses—switching either to zone or to multiple defenses. (By multiple defenses we mean the continual switching from man-for-man to various zone defensive alignments.)

The effectiveness of our man-for-man attack has encouraged opponents to use zone defenses against us; we also feel there are other basic reasons for the increased use of zones. These are: (1) that the individual offensive player has become too highly skilled to be handled by one defensive player; (2) that man-for-man team offenses in general have become too complex to be contained without excessive scouting techniques and considerable time devoted in practice sessions to handling specific offensive maneuvers; (3) that the increased popularity of the zone press has necessitated the use of the zone defense as the back-up defense; and (4) the increased size of the individual players themselves has made the zone defense stronger, since teams may then keep their big men near the basket where they are most effective.

As a result of the increasing number of zone defense teams that we encountered, it was felt that an effective zone offense that would comply with the Trident strategy and permit an easy transition from the man-for-man attack to the zone attack was a must for a complete offensive arsenal. This would then prevent teams from changing defenses to reduce the effectiveness of the man-for-man attack. In other words, if we didn't have an effective zone attack, our opponents would play zone defenses against us.

TRIDENT ZONE PRINCIPLES

Even though the philosophy of zone defenses is completely different from that of the basic man-for-man defenses, we kept in mind the basic power factors of the Trident strategy in developing our zone attack. The following rules and attitudes are indispensable to the successful operation of the zone offense:

1. The coach must possess and develop in his players a positive attitude toward breaking the zone.

2. Spot shooting drills must be run every night as part of the organized practice. Shots should be taken *only* from the corners and the sides of the arc at the foul line during the drill. (See Chapter 11, Diagram 11-7.)

3. Every player must be a scoring threat.

4. Offensive rebound position to get the maximum

number of second shots is part of the pattern and is not left to chance.

5. Speed in moving the ball is a must unless opponents overplay passing lanes. The five man circle passing drill should be used to demonstrate to the players the proper speed and type of pass that they should strive for. (See Chapter 11, Diagram 11-20.)

6. Players should be taught the reasons for the drills and patterns so they can better understand and attain the prescribed objectives.

We would like to reiterate the importance of principles numbers 1 and 4. It has been our experience that teams that have had a positive attitude concerning zone defenses have been most effective in defeating them. We believe in the idea that if opponents have to change defenses because they are unable to stop a certain portion of our offense, they are at a psychological disadvantage. Our players firmly believe that they can defeat either man-for-man or zone defenses.

The value of principle number four has been discussed earlier in the book but should be re-emphasized again in relation to the zone offense. Against zone defenses it becomes even more difficult to obtain the back door rebound position, since achieving this position depends to a great extent upon the individual players' abilities to maneuver into the proper area. The main reason that the proper back door position is harder to obtain is that the defensive men are reacting to the movement of the ball rather than the individual players, and thus it is more difficult to catch a player out of position.

Since it is somewhat more difficult to obtain the inside position for rebounding against zones, we believe that more emphasis must be placed upon the importance of the back door position. The players responsible for back door rebounding must be drilled on individual techniques that will improve their rebound positioning and, as a result, give the team more of those vital second shots.

Most of our players develop their own individual techniques which are effective for them, and in which they have confidence. However, every player should be familiar with two sound techniques for obtaining inside position. These are: (1) the baseline slide (Photo Series 6-1 to 6-5), and (2) the reverse pivot pin (Photo Series 6-6 to 6-10). As can be seen, we devote a great deal of time to obtaining the second shot in all of our patterns, as this is critical to the successful use of the Trident strategy.

Photo 6–1. *The baseline slide. Defensive man 42 (white uniform) starts to box out offensive man 33 (dark uniform).*

Photo 6–2. *Offensive player starts his baseline slide by squeezing in along the base line.*

Photo 6–3. *Offensive player slides to inside position.*'

Photo 6–4. *Once inside, offensive player must continue to maneuver so that he is not pushed too far under the basket.*

Photo 6–5. *Offensive player has now secured inside position and obtained the rebound.*

Photo 6–6. *The reverse pivot pin. Defensive man 42 (white uniform) starts to box out but he is aware that he was beaten by the baseline slide.*

Photo 6–7. *Defensive man 42 is still boxing out and is determined to stop the baseline slide.*

Photo 6–8. *Offensive center 33 feels the pressure from the box out and starts his reverse pivot.*

Photo 6–9. *Offensive center 33 now attempts to pin the defensive center behind him.*

Photo 6–10. *The offensive center, having gained inside position, now clears the rebound.*

REGULAR

Since most teams that we play are familiar with the pressure we exert on the basket area as a result of the Trident's man-for-man patterns, when they go to a zone defense it is primarily to plug up the inside to prevent penetration of both the ball and the players. Consequently, we have found that in order to draw out the defense we must first establish our outside zone attack. This means that first we will use what we call our "Regular" zone pattern. It is our belief that one of the most difficult areas of the floor to cover with a zone defense is the corner area. We know that if a zone defense wishes to stop the shot from this area, they must move one of their defensive men to the corner. This then has the effect of pulling the zone out of shape and easing the congestion either under the basket or in the high post. Also, many coaches still believe that the corner shot is one of the poorest shots in basketball, and they are reluctant to have their men play the corner shooter aggressively.

For these reasons, our first attempt to score over the zone or from the outside is with the corner shot.

At this point many coaches may lose interest in this chapter and turn to the next, feeling that any zone attack that runs a pattern just to obtain a corner shot against a zone defense cannot be *his* answer to a zone offense. Here we would like to emphasize the four things that we do to make this pattern highly successful.

First is the development of a positive psychological outlook in our players that the corner shot is an effective weapon. We inform them that many teams are reluctant to defend properly against this shot and that if they do take the shot away from us we then will have weakened their defense in other areas. We even go so far as to tell our players that they are ordered to shoot from the corner whenever they have an open shot. We tell them that we, the coaches, take full responsibility and that their only job is to take open shots and make the basket. We have found many of our players actually hoping that teams will play zone so that they may run our "Regular" zone pattern.

Second is the diligent practice time spent with the spot shooting drill that has been mentioned earlier. As you know, we spend time in every practice session on this drill and that two of our four spots are the corners. Players can be drilled so that they have the same confidence in these shots as they would have in free throws and many will develop a comparable shooting percentage from these areas.

Third is the speed drill we run for this pattern (Chapter 11). We spend some time in every practice session running this pattern so that the ball movement, timing, and shot become a simple reflex action. We emphasize this point so much that we do not allow our players to dribble closer to the basket for a shot, even when a closer shot presents itself. We do not want any indecision on their part. If they are open in the corner we want that shot because we have spent many hours practicing it.

Fourth, we tell our players that should they happen to miss a shot we still have an outstanding chance to get the rebound and the second shot, as we will have our two best rebounders in the prime rebounding positions—namely, the back door and center positions.

To begin "Regular" our offensive alignment is the same as for any of our other patterns. We key the pattern with the call "Regular" by the guard moving the ball into the front court. We have found, however, that most of the time it is not necessary to call "Regular" because this is generally the first zone pattern we use. As 1 moves into the offensive area, 3 again does his homework and breaks for the ball. We would like to have him receive the ball a little deeper than the foul line extended (Diagram 6-1). This is to try to get the baseline defensive man, in this case X5, to defend 3. 1 should then make his pass to the outside shoulder of 3 to keep the ball away from 3's defensive man and begin his cut across the top half of the free throw circle. Usually 1 will throw a direct pass if 3's defensive man is not pressuring him.

As 3 receives the ball 5 drops down the lane attempting to get the defensive man responsible for defending the deep lane area on his back, in this case X4 (Diagram 6-2). If we have been successful in getting X5 to defend against 3 when he receives the ball, and if 5 has been successful in getting good body position on X4, 3 should then pass the ball to 5 to attempt to get the inside basket. 4 and 1 must both be alert to the pass from 3 to 5 since they will then become responsible for the back door and middle rebounding positions. Here again let us stress that even though this is basically our outside pattern we still attempt to threaten the basket. This has the effect of making a sagging zone retreat toward the basket even more.

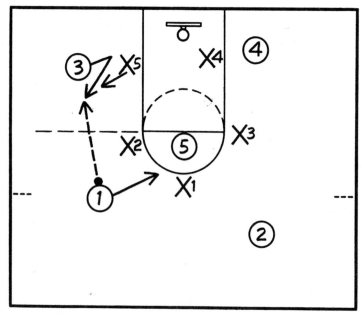

Diagram 6–1

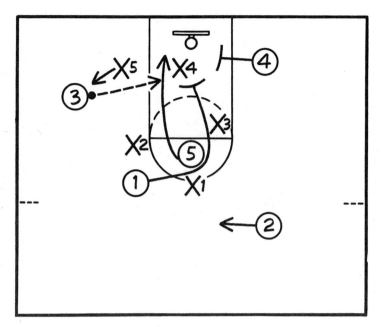

Diagram 6-2

If, in order to stop our first attempt to get the ball inside to 5, X4 successfully fronts 5, 3 then quickly reverses the ball by passing to 2 who makes himself available by moving toward the ball (Diagram 6-3). 1 continues his cut across the foul circle and into the opposite corner. Here he should line himself up so that he is even with the basket and above a line extending from the backboard. 1 should then turn to face the basket so that when he receives the ball he will be in proper shooting position. 4, meanwhile, moves to an area near the junction of the foul line and foul circle so as to be able to move quickly to receive the ball.

If 5 does not receive the ball as he drops down the foul lane, he then positions himself in the low post area on the same side of the lane as 3. His main job now becomes the obtaining of the back door rebound position when the shot is taken.

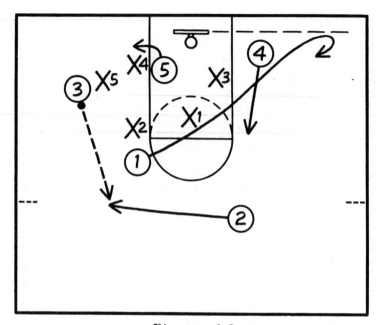

Diagram 6-3

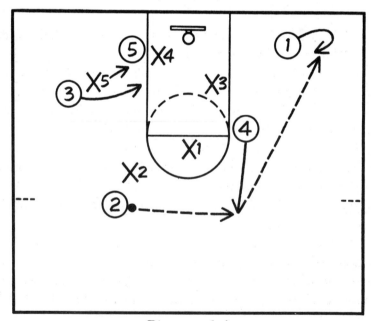

Diagram 6-4

As 2 receives the ball from 3, 4 breaks to an open area near the top of the foul circle. 4's job is to be sure that he is available as soon as 2 receives the pass so that 2 may quickly pass him the ball. 4 immediately looks to see if 1 is open and if he is, passes the ball quickly to him for the corner shot (Diagram 6-4). 3 and 5, meanwhile, move into a position to be able to readily obtain the inside rebound position.

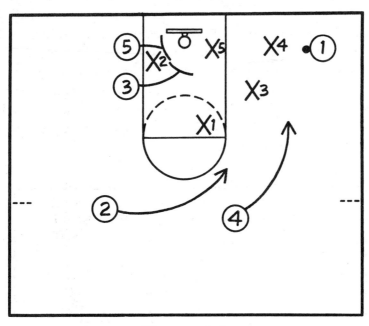

Diagram 6–5

As 1 receives the ball, both 3 and 5 obtain the inside rebound position since they are expecting 1 to shoot if he is open. 4 and 2 have both followed their passes, expecting a return pass (Diagram 6-5).

If 1 is being pressured by X4 so that he cannot take a shot without forcing it, he may then return the ball to 4, who is generally open for a shot, since X3 will usually try to sag to fill the hole left by X4, who has been pulled out of position by 1 in the corner. This maneuver occasionally occurs after we have run our "Regular" pattern a few times and 1 has scored.

If, when 4 receives the ball from 1 he cannot shoot, it is usually because X3 has decided not to sag to fill the hole created by X4, but to prevent the shot by 4. This then will leave a hole in the deep post position into which we break 5 (Diagram 6-7). 4 then passes the ball inside to 5 for the close-in shot at the basket. Also, as 5 breaks for the ball, 3 clears the lane by moving to the back door area vacated by 5. 3 now becomes responsible for the back door rebound position.

If 4 cannot shoot and cannot pass the ball in to 5, it could mean that X1 has sagged all the way from his point position to help cover 5 (Diagram 6-8). If this occurs, 4 should simply pass the ball to 2 who should be wide open for an easy shot from our spot shooting area.

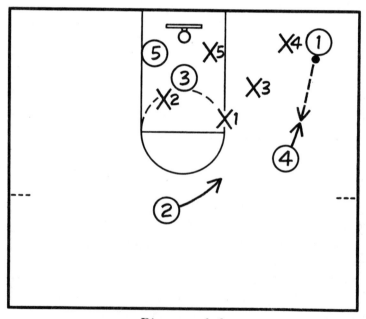

Diagram 6–6

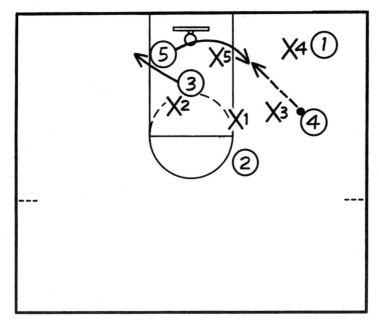

Diagram 6-7

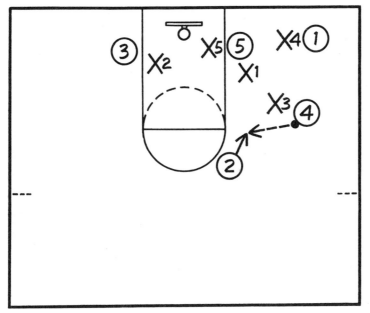

Diagram 6-8

If X1 has not sagged to prevent the pass inside to 5 and X3 is still defensing 4 so he cannot shoot, it will probably be X4 who has dropped inside to help cover (Diagram 6-9). In this case, 4 should then return the ball to 1 who will then be open for his corner shot. 3, however, will have the back door responsibility and 5 will work for the middle position.

It should also be kept in mind that the players may reset the pattern again or change to still a different pattern if they feel the defense is not responding to the pattern. The guards may do this by simply demanding the ball and setting up our basic alignment.

SHORT CIRCUIT

As stated before, the "Regular" pattern depends to a large degree upon the ability of the offense to move the ball quickly

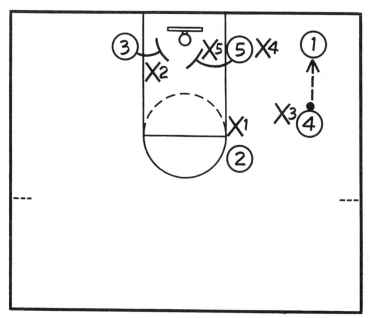

Diagram 6–9

and safely from one side of the court to the other. This is, of course, quite easily accomplished when the zone defense is very compact. If the zone is very aggressive, we generally use our inside pattern which we will discuss in the next chapter. However, we have found that some teams will attempt to play a compact or sagging zone defense with their back men, but use their point man to chase the ball, jump passing lanes, and in general be extremely aggressive.

It is when we play a team that has an active point man that we use our "Short Circuit" option of our "Regular" zone pattern.

The pattern begins exactly like the basic "Regular" pattern with 1 passing to 3 and cutting across the top of the foul circle. 5 drops down the lane and if he is open will receive the ball. 4 moves to an area near the junction of the foul

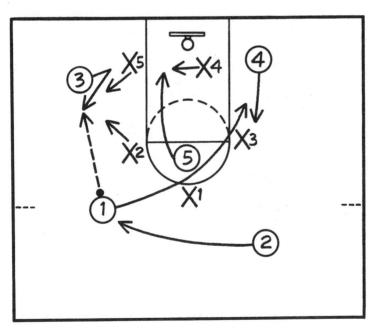

Diagram 6-10

circle and the foul line and 2 moves across the court to be available for a pass from 3 (Diagram 6-10).

If, however, 5 is not open to receive a pass from 3, 3 must then reverse the ball to 2 to attempt to get the corner shot by 1. It is at this point that most of the teams that employ the chasing point man will use him to attempt to stop the pass to 2 and thus prevent the ball from being reversed to the corner (Diagram 6-11). It is then that we run the "Short Circuit" option.

The "Short Circuit" maneuver is not keyed by a call but is run automatically when the point defensive man, X1, jumps the passing lane. 4, who has moved into the area near the foul line, now breaks directly across the foul lane into an open area to receive a pass from 3. 3 then passes the ball to 4, who may either shoot if he is open or pass the ball to 1 for the corner

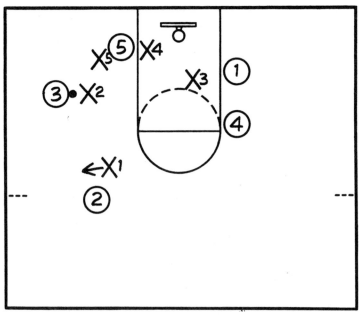

Diagram 6-11

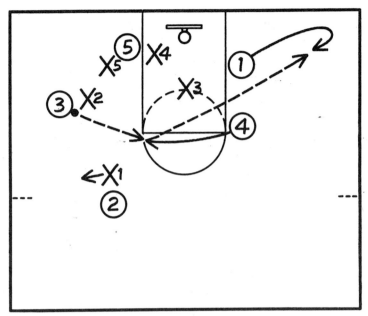

Diagram 6–12

shot (Diagram 6-12). Thus, 4 is able to take advantage of the open area created by X1 when he attempts to intercept the pass from 3 to 2.

We have found that many teams will vary their defensive strategy by having their point man only occasionally jump the passing lane. As a result, we have added one defensive man to our speed drill for the "Regular" zone offense. We then have this man play the point position and vary his defensive procedure by occasionally jumping the passing lane. This then aids 4 in determining when to run the "Short Circuit" option and when to run the basic "Regular" attack.

7

The Trident Inside Zone Attack

The inside zone attack is used to complement our "Regular" or outside zone attack offense. This inside attack differs in the way we attempt to defeat a zone defense. There are four basic reasons why we use our "Overload" or inside attack.

First, we find it to be useful against very aggressive zone defenses that like to pressure both the men and the ball by jumping passing lanes. This makes any inside attack much more effective since the defense must necessarily gamble to be effective which leaves many opportunities for the offense to move the ball into openings created by the defense. As we have stated in the previous chapter, we use our outside attack to encourage the sagging zone defense teams to overplay our passing lanes and thus create the openings inside that will allow us to penetrate the periphery of this defense.

Second, we use it as a change of pace from our "Regular" attack, since we emphasize the importance of rapid ball movement in our outside attack to make it most effective; in our inside attack we stress the importance of accuracy and penetration of the defense with the ball. We still like to move the ball as quickly as possible; however, we want accuracy at all costs even at the expense of rapid ball movement. Since we place such a high premium upon accuracy we have experienced a rather marked slowdown of the ball as well as an increase in the time necessary to get the open shot. In this way we are able to throw off the timing of the zone defense's movement and control the tempo of the game in general. This is especially important when the opponents catch fire and go on a hot shooting streak.

Third, in combating 2-1-2 or 2-3 zone defenses, we feel that it enables us to move the ball inside against these particular zones or force them to overshift their zone alignment to stop penetration of the ball. If they do not overshift we attempt to move the ball inside, and if they do overshift we quickly move the ball to the weak side for a medium-range jump shot. The inside attack is most effective against 2-1-2 and 2-3 zones but can be used against 1-2-2 zones also.

Fourth, we use it to reduce the effects of a bad shooting night. As all coaches know, this happens to all teams occasionally during the season and as such every coach must recognize this and change his strategy accordingly. We feel that due to the emphasis placed upon spot shooting we should have a minimum number of these so-called "bad" nights. However, when this happens we attempt to use our inside pattern as much as possible so that we can work for the highest percentage shot available. We still do not use the inside pattern exclusively, just as we do not use the outside pattern all the time. However, we will tell our guards which of the patterns they should run the majority of the time.

OVERLOADED DIAMOND POWER PLAY

The word we use to key our basic inside zone attack is "Overload." This simply means that we go into our basic "Overloaded Diamond" formation (Diagram 7-1). This formation, of course, can be moved to either side of the floor.

Again our pattern is started from our basic alignment and is keyed by the guard who advances the ball into the front court by the call "Overload." To start the pattern, 1 passes the ball to 3 and again cuts across the top of the foul circle (Diagram 7-2).

3 should still attempt to receive the ball below the foul line extended to encourage X3 to leave the baseline area to defend against 3's shot. 5 then slides down the foul lane attempting to get X5 on his back. If this happens, 3 should pass the ball to 5 who is tight to the basket for an easy hook shot

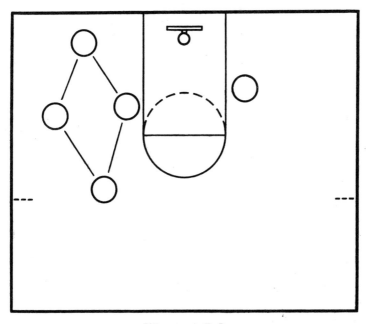

Diagram 7-1

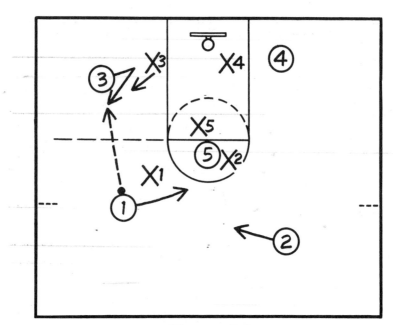

Diagram 7-2

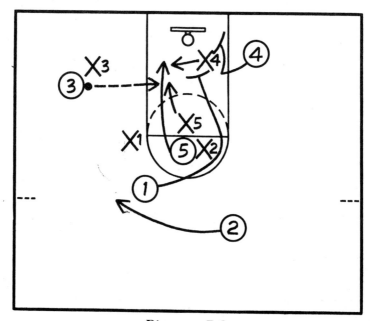

Diagram 7-3

or other scoring move (Diagram 7-3). As the pass goes into 5, 4 maneuvers for the middle rebound area and 1 works for the back door rebound responsibility. 2 continues to have defensive responsibility but slides to the point area on the same side as the ball. As you can see, our first maneuver to get the ball inside is exactly the same as the first option in "Regular."

If when 5 drops down the lane he is not open, he continues to the base line on the same side as the ball (Diagram 7-4). His responsibility here is to remain even with the basket (not behind the backboard) no closer to the corner than the midpoint between the corner and the basket and facing both the ball and the basket.

As 5 clears the lane going halfway to the corner, 4 breaks toward the ball and an open area alongside the lane. If 4 is open, 3 passes him the ball (Diagram 7-5).

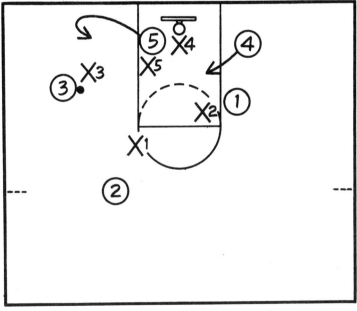

Diagram 7–4

As 4 receives the ball, he should turn toward the base line to face the basket and become a threat to score. If he is open, he should shoot as 1 moves to obtain the back door rebound position (Diagram 7-6).

Again let us re-emphasize the importance of 4 turning toward the base line if at all possible to become a scoring threat. This now gives 4 several options. His first option as we have already shown is to shoot if he is open. Usually, however, the defense will gang up on 4, making a good shot difficult but freeing other offensive players. As 4 turns toward the base line he places pressure on X5 who will usually drop off 5 on the base line to help stop 4 from either driving or shooting. If as 4 turns he sees X5 moving to help defense him, he should drop the ball off to 5 who begins a baseline cut toward the basket (Diagram 7-7).

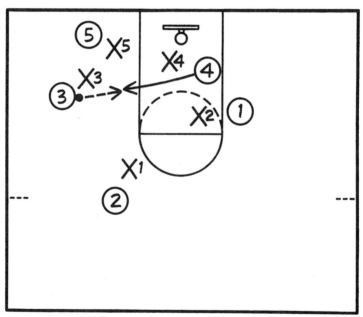

Diagram 7–5

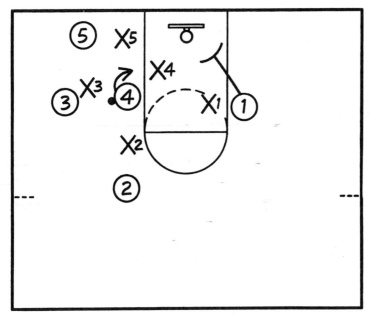

Diagram 7–6

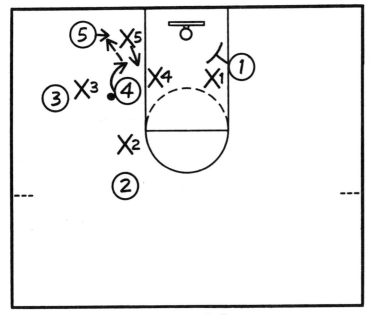

Diagram 7–7

If when 4 receives the ball and begins his baseline turn, he is double teamed by X3, 4 may return the ball to 3 who drifts toward the base line a little to receive the ball more easily and to be freer for the shot (Diagram 7-8).

If 4 receives the ball and is double teamed by X2, he should pass the ball to 2 who has moved to a spot shooting area near the side of the lane (Diagram 7-9).

2 may have this same shot at the side of the lane available to him when 3 has the ball if X2 sags to prevent the pass to 4 (Diagram 7-10). Usually, however, if a defensive team begins to sag their front line men that much, our guards will automatically go to our "Regular" or outside zone attack to force them to become more aggressive.

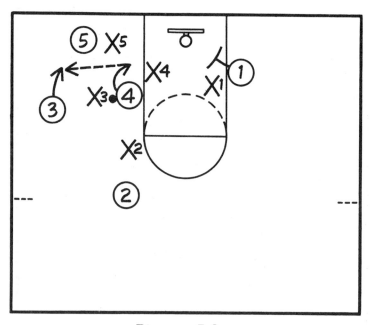

Diagram 7–8

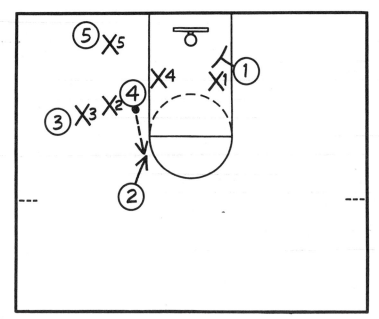

Diagram 7–9

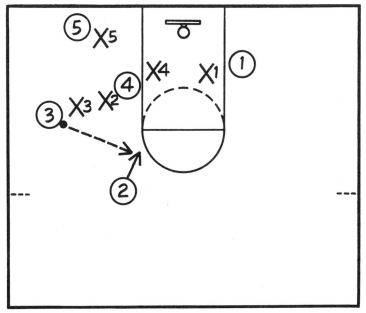

Diagram 7–10

If 3 feels he cannot make a safe pass to 4, his second choice will usually be 5 on the base line (Diagram 7-11). 5's position should be even with the basket, no more than halfway between the basket and the sideline, feet on the floor, knees flexed, and facing so he can see both the ball and the basket. This position permits him to take a quick, yet accurate shot should he be open.

As 5 receives the ball from 3, 4 again turns toward the base line and attempts to get X4 on his back as he slides toward the basket. If he is successful, 5 will pass 4 the ball for the easy score (Diagram 7-12). 1 again moves to obtain the back door rebound position.

If 5 finds that X5 is beginning to cheat a little to try to prevent the pass to 4, he may then fake the pass to 4 and take the shot himself (Diagram 7-13).

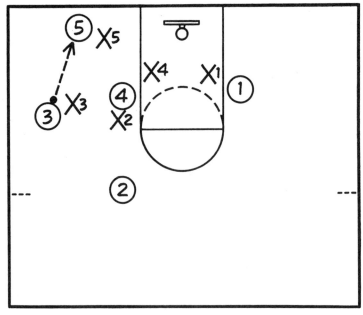

Diagram 7-11

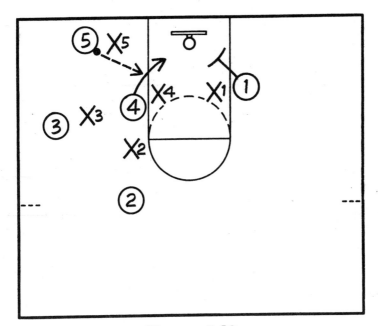

Diagram 7-12

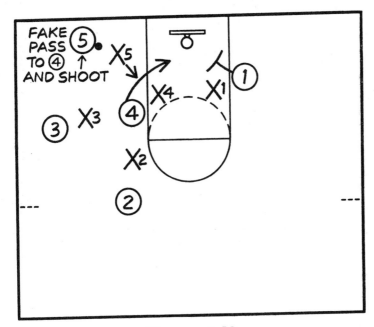

Diagram 7-13

There is one other maneuver in the "Overload" Power Attack that we use when 4 is being overplayed to the baseline side. As we have indicated, we want 4 to turn toward the base line whenever possible and as a result some defenses will attempt to prevent this move by playing X4 on the baseline side of 4 (Diagram 7-14).

When this occurs, 4 may pivot away from the base line when he receives the ball. He may then either take a hook shot, jump shot, or drive to the basket if he is open (Diagram 7-15).

If, as 4 pivots to threaten the basket, he is double teamed by X1, from behind he should drop the ball off to 1 for the easy score (Diagram 7-16).

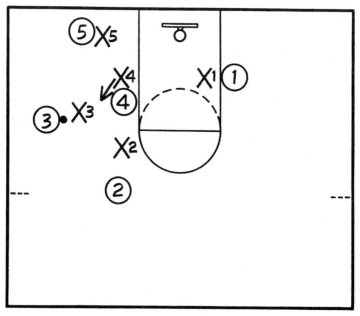

Diagram 7-14

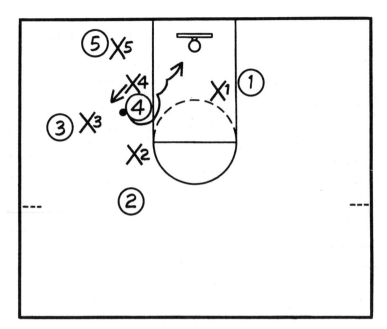

Diagram 7–15

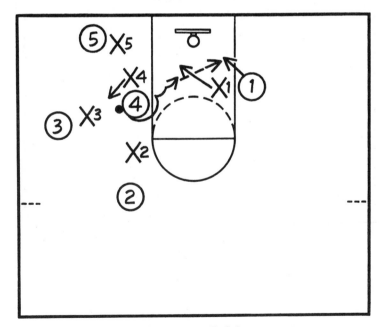

Diagram 7–16

OVERLOADED DIAMOND—WEAKSIDE PLAY

The weakside play of the "Overloaded Diamond" can be used against any type of zone defense quite effectively. We usually use this against defensive teams that try to match up their men against us or attempt to sag a great deal on our "Overloaded Diamond Power Play." This play allows us to do two important things.

First, it permits us to isolate one of our best shooters in a one-on-one situation within 20 feet of the basket and second, it permits us to have our best rebounders available near the basket.

The play is initiated by our point guard, in this case 2, whenever he receives the ball (Diagram 7-17). As 2 receives the ball, 1 breaks toward him expecting to receive the pass in the weakside spot shooting area near the junction of the foul line and the foul circle. If he is open, he may take the shot immediately or attempt to quickly outmaneuver X1 for the shot. Here let us note that the maneuver used by 1 must be done quickly while he is still isolated in the one-on-one situation.

As 1 receives the ball, he turns to be a threat to score and 4 attempts to obtain a position in front of X4 as he drops diagonally across the lane toward the basket (Diagram 7-18). If 1 is not free for the shot when he receives the ball, it usually means that X1 is playing him rather close. This may then leave an alley or opening behind X1 so that 1 may make a quick pass inside to 4. 5 and 3 then have the responsibility for the back door and middle rebound positions. 2 continues to have defensive responsibility and slowly begins to drift to the ball side of the floor after passing to 1.

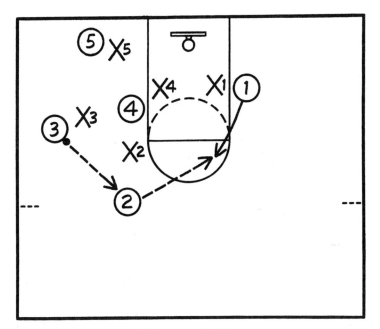

Diagram 7-17

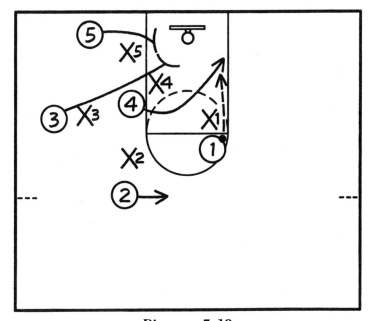

Diagram 7-18

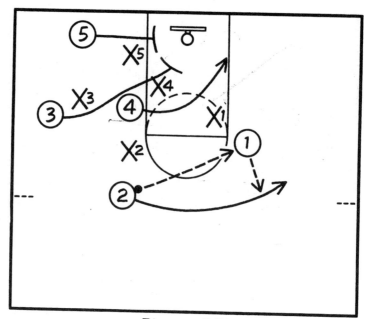

Diagram 7–19

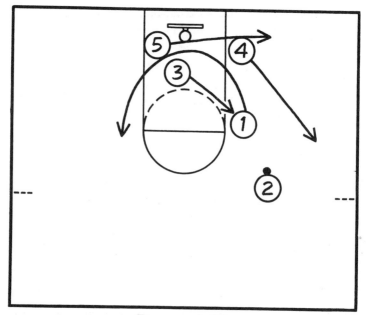

Diagram 7–20

SWING-IT

"Swing-it" is not another play but simply refers to our moving the overload from one side of the floor to the other. We mention it here because we swing our overload to the opposite side after an attempt to use the "Weakside Play." There are two ways that we key the cross court movement.

The first key is an automatic one. We "Swing-it" every time 2 passes the ball to 1 in an attempt to use the "Weakside Play." If 1 is not able to pass the ball to 4 as he makes his diagonal cut or if 1 is not free for the shot, he will then return the ball to 2 as 2 moves across the top of the foul circle (Diagram 7-19).

As the ball is returned to 2 by 1, 4 breaks to the wing area, 3 moves to the high post, and 5 moves to the baseline position, again no more than halfway to the corner (Diagram 7-20). 1 then makes a deep cut to the basket before moving to the weak side.

The "Overloaded Diamond" has now been moved across the floor with 2 in possession of the ball (Diagram 7-21). It is at this point that we add an additional rotation by the guards. 2 may now pass the ball to 4 and cut behind 3 to the weak side, and 1 fills his position at the point. We do this to get more player movement and also to permit both our guards to be the weakside guard.

The second key is used if 2 wishes to "Swing-it" but is not able to pass the ball to 1 because the defense is jumping the passing lane (Diagram 7-22). 2 may then dribble the ball across the court. The dribble tells the players that 2 wants to "Swing-it" and they move to their new positions. 4 cuts from the high post to the opposite wing position, 3 to the high post, 5 cuts the base line to the opposite baseline position, and 1 moves to the weak side.

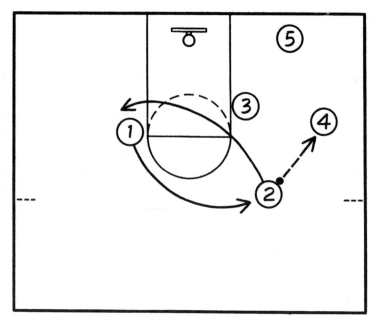

Diagram 7-21

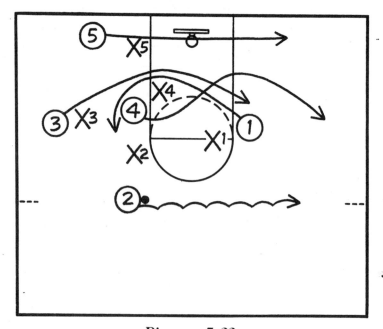

Diagram 7-22

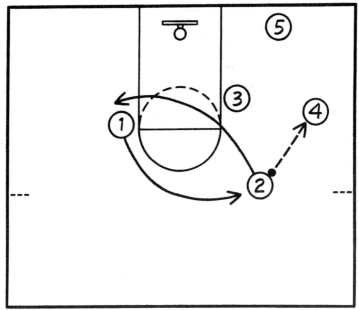

Diagram 7–23

2 may again pass the ball to 4 and then cut to the weak side (Diagram 7-23). 1 will then fill the point position. The dribble key thus permits us to "Swing" the overload even though the defense overplays our passing lanes.

BUTTONHOOK

"Buttonhook" is another setup of the "Overloaded Diamond" pattern. In this pattern we still have the same basic positions on the floor but change the personnel to obtain better rebounding or better shooting. We also use this pattern when teams play a "Box and One" defense on our center, 5. This is quite similar to a 2-1-2 zone alignment except that 5's defensive man, X5, plays 5 wherever he goes and attempts to keep the ball from him. We then play 5 in the prime rebounding area, the "back door," which reduces the effectiveness of this special coverage.

The pattern is keyed again by the guard moving the ball into the front court and calling, "Buttonhook." 1 then passes the ball to 3 and begins his cut across the top of the foul circle as 5 drops down the lane looking for a pass from 3 (Diagram 7-24). As can be seen, the "Buttonhook" option begins with much the same maneuver as all our other options.

It is at this point that the center, 5, and the guard, 1, change positions by "Buttonhooking" into each other's position (Diagram 7-25). 4 again cuts to the high post area and 2 fills the point position. This now gives us better shooting and passing in the baseline position and better rebounding in the "back door" area.

Also, as was mentioned before, if a team plays a "Box and One" defense against 5 it puts X3 in the very difficult position of having to try to cover both 3 and 1 (Diagram 7-26) or X4

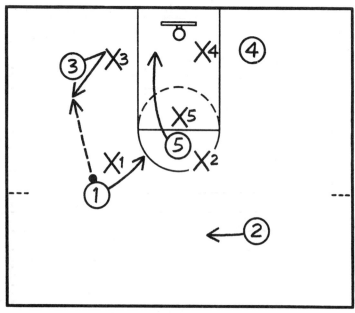

Diagram 7–24

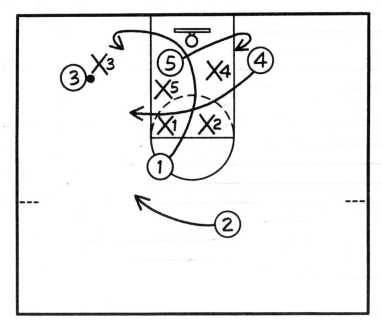

Diagram 7–25

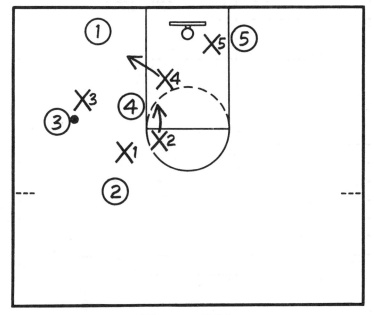

Diagram 7–26

may move to cover 1 which then puts a front line defensive man on 4 in the high post.

The "Buttonhook" option also has the "Weakside Play" which is now run with 5 receiving the ball from 2 (Diagram 7-27).

Again we can "Swing-it" to the other side of the floor by having 5 return the ball to 2 if he cannot shoot or pass to 4 on the diagonal cut (Diagram 7-28).

2 may now pass to 4 and then make the "Buttonhook" cut to become the new baseline man (Diagram 7-29). 1 fills in the point position for him, 3 moves to the high post area, and 5 moves again to the "back door" rebound position.

2 may still "Swing" the "Buttonhook" option by again using the dribble as a key if he is unable to pass the ball to 5 (Diagram 7-30). As soon as 2 begins the dribble, 5 cuts to

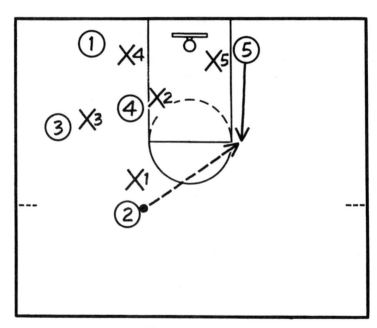

Diagram 7–27

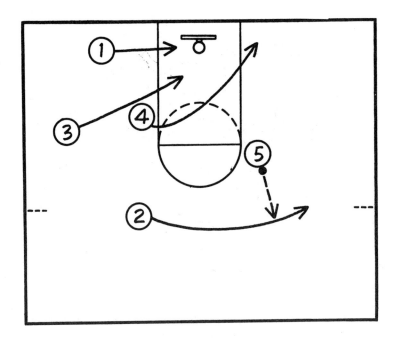

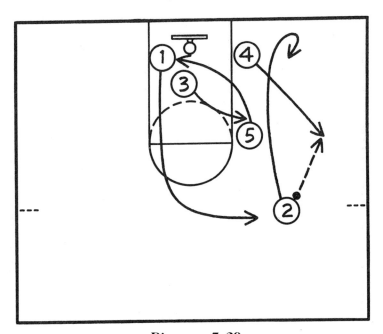

Diagram 7-29

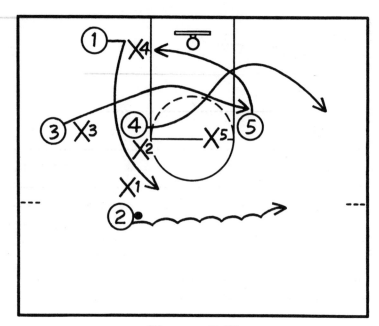

Diagram 7–30

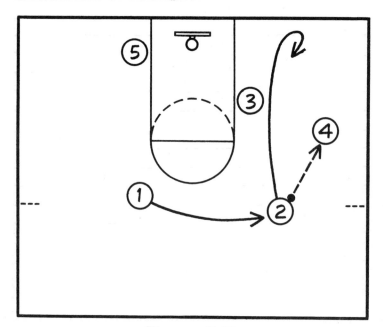

Diagram 7–31

the "back door," 4 moves to the wing position, 3 to the high post area, and 1 to the top of the foul circle.

2 again passes to 4 and "Buttonhooks" to the base line, and 1 fills the point position (Diagram 7-31).

ATTACKING THE NOTCH

The zone patterns and options already mentioned, we use against all zone defenses; however, we use a 2-1-2 alignment against most teams that employ a 1-3-1 zone defense. This 2-1-2 attack we refer to as "Attacking the Notch." In this alignment we do not move our men too much but attempt to work the ball quickly and accurately for the high percentage shot.

This pattern may be keyed by any of our players as soon as they realize that the defense being used against them is a

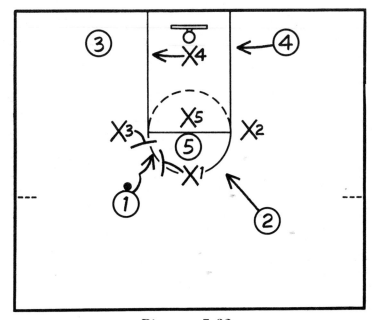

Diagram 7-32

1-3-1 zone by simply calling out 2-1-2 or "Attack the Notch." On the call, the guard with the ball, in this case 1, dribbles toward the foul circle at a point between the defensive men X3 and X1. This is the area we refer to as the "notch" (Diagram 7-32). 1's first duty is to become a threat to score, and we permit our guards to shoot whenever they can reach the foul circle and have an open shot. Most defenses, of course, will not permit this shot and many will attempt to trap 1 with both X1 and X3.

As soon as the defense begins to move toward 1 and he realizes that he will not have the good shot, his first option is to look for 4 who is moving toward the basket (Diagram 7-33). If 4 is open, 1 should throw him a quick, high pass that X5 cannot intercept.

If 4 is not open, it may be because X4 has not moved to the ball side of the floor but has held his position. 1 should then pass the ball to 3 for the medium-range jump shot. 3's position should be facing both the ball and the basket with knees flexed. This permits 3 to take a quick, yet accurate shot. We also allow 3 and 4 to operate only within 15 feet of the basket. This makes them a scoring threat at all times (Diagram 7-34).

1 still has another option available to him if he finds both 4 and 3 covered. This usually means that X4 has moved to the ball side of the floor to defend against 3, and X2 has dropped down the lane to defend against 4 (Diagram 7-35). 1 may now pass the ball to 2, who has remained a step behind 1 to permit a better passing angle. 2 may then take a quick dribble to the spot shooting area near the junction of the foul line and the foul circle for the high percentage shot.

It has been our experience that nearly all 1-3-1 zone defenses encounter difficulty in effectively stopping this attack.

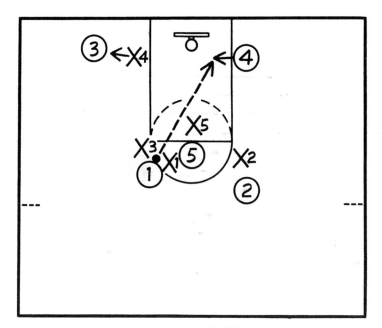

Diagram 7–33

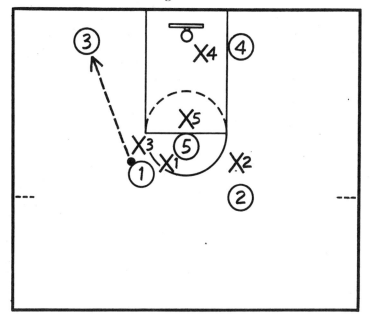

Diagram 7–34

HELPFUL HINTS IN TEACHING THE TRIDENT

1. In Chapter 6 we discussed the "Short Circuit" option of the "Regular" zone pattern. It is important to remember that whenever 4 decides to use the "Short Circuit" maneuver he should remain in the high post area. Then if a shot does not immediately develop, the team is automatically in an "Overloaded Diamond" and continues with this inside attack until a shot is obtained or the guards decide to reset the offense.

2. Remember that the men playing the baseline position in the "Overloaded Diamond" or the "Attacking the Notch" pattern may never go beyond a point midway between the basket and the corner of the court.

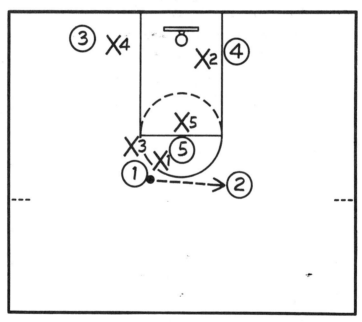

Diagram 7–35

8

What the Trident Does
Against Pressure Defenses

The popularity of the pressure defenses today has forced all coaches to prepare their teams for them. These defenses are of various types and include everything from full-court, man-for-man and zone press pressure to half-court, man-for-man and chase defenses. In this chapter, however, we would like to limit our discussion to half-court pressure defenses and the way we attack them.

Probably the most important defensive technique used today is the "changing defense" idea. By this we mean that teams will often change their type or style of defense every time they come down the floor. Because this technique can be highly confusing, we feel that the offense you use must be adaptable to these changes. Considerable time and effort must be given to teaching your players to recognize the defense they are meeting and to adapt their offensive attack to meet it.

To simplify the process of recognizing half-court pressure defenses we tell our players that they all fall into one of two categories. These are man-for-man pressure and zone pressure. All defenses that attack the offensive man with the ball with only one player we label as man-for-man defenses, and all those that attack the ball with more than one defensive player we call zone defenses. As a result of this rule we have made the offensive players' job very simple and they will know what avenues of attack are open to them.

Since the majority of half-court pressure defenses you meet are of the man-for-man variety we would like to discuss them first. Generally the teams that employ the man-for-man pressure will meet your guards approximately at the ten-second line and will overplay the passing lanes to the center and forward on the same side of the floor (Diagram 8-1).

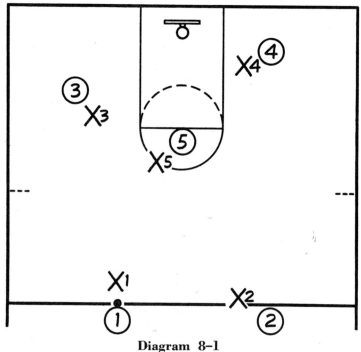

Diagram 8-1

We have found that the most effective pattern against the man-for-man pressure defense has been the Direct Pass Pattern of the Trident Offense. Because of this we attempt to run the regular Direct Pass Pattern against all man-for-man pressure defenses if they will let us. By this we mean that many pressure defenses are really semi-pressure defenses that only attempt to force your offensive men somewhat farther from the basket before allowing them to handle the ball. If this is the situation, we continue to run the Direct Pass Pattern beginning it at the ten-second line and attempting to get the ball to 1 or 2 as they break free from their men on the give-and-go or rub-off maneuvers (Diagram 8-2).

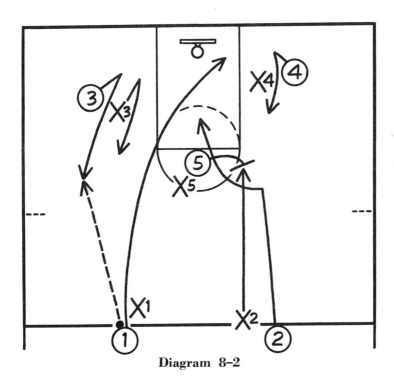

Diagram 8–2

ROTATION

We have found that if a man-for-man pressure defense team allows us to make the pass from 1 to 3, they will be giving us many high percentage shots including lay-ins. Be sure then before trying anything else against man-for-man pressure, that you cannot consistently make the pass from 1 to 3.

If, however, we find that our opponents are playing a "hard-nosed," true, man-for-man pressure defense that contests every pass, we then have our ball handling guard call "rotation." We usually like to have 1 wait on this call until he sees 3 attempt to break clear for the ball as in the regular Direct Pass Pattern. 1 must keep his dribble going and as soon

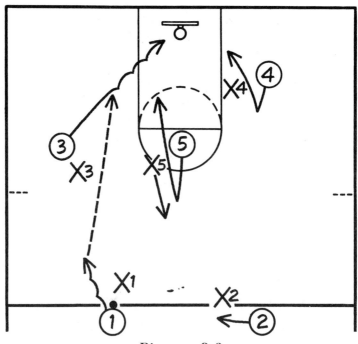

Diagram 8–3

as he realizes X3 will not allow the pass to 3 he makes his call, "rotation." 1 then dribbles toward 3's forward position looking for 3 as he cuts to the basket (Diagram 8-3). If 3 is open, 1 passes him the ball and 5 and 4 quickly work for rebound position.

If 3 does not receive the pass from 1, he continues under the basket and takes 4's forward position. 1 then continues his dribble to 3's position, while 4 rotates to take 2's guard spot. 2 now becomes the first cutter just as in the regular Direct Pass Pattern. If his defensive man plays him normally, that is between 2 and the basket, 2 then cuts in front of him as he goes to the basket (Diagram 8-4). 1 then follows his pass to 2, expecting a return pass.

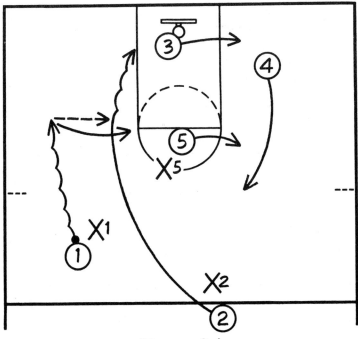

Diagram 8-4

If X2, however, continues to play between 2 and the ball, 2 should then make a quick cut behind X2 and go to the basket (Diagram 8-5). 1 again should follow his pass, expecting the ball to be returned to him.

If 2 does not get the ball, he continues to cut beneath the basket and back to the guard position with defensive responsibilities. 4 now becomes the second cutter and rubs off X4 on the center, 5. 1 then passes the ball to 4 and follows the pass, expecting a return (Diagram 8-6). If 4 does not receive the ball, he continues to the near side of the foul lane to get rebound position.

As 5 catches X4 on the rub-off he delays momentarily. He then pivots in the direction X4 attempts to go and drops down the back side of the foul lane to obtain the back door rebound position. 3 brushes X3 off on 5 and cuts to receive the ball near the foul line. 3 may now shoot, pass to 5 in a high-low maneuver, or reverse his direction and drive X3 to the basket (Diagram 8-7).

As you can see, the "rotation" option is the Direct Pass Pattern of the Trident Offense. The only real difference is that the second cutter, in this case 4, does not return to the guard position but stays in to rebound. The "rotation" option may be used at any time; however, it is most helpful when the forwards are being overplayed by their defensive men.

Earlier we stated that we categorized pressure defenses into two types: man-for-man and zones. We also stated that any defense that attacked the ball with two or more defensive men is classified as a zone. Our reason for this is that regardless of the type of coverage the opponents use, as soon as they attempt to double team one man they have left one offensive man free. This means that if the free man gets the ball, someone will have to leave his own man to cover him or let him score, unless the team has some sort of zone arrangement to handle the situation.

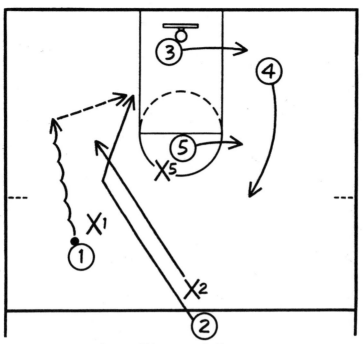

Diagram 8-5

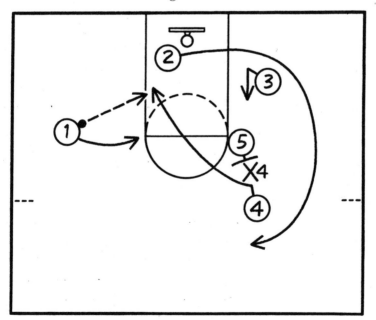

Diagram 8-6

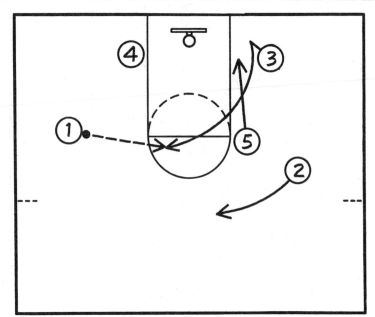

Diagram 8–7

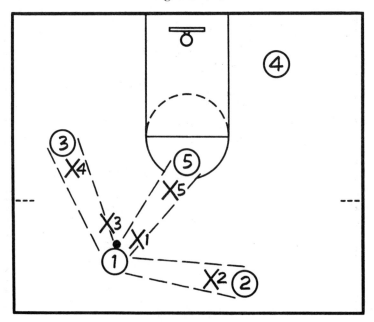

Diagram 8–8

Our aim is to penetrate the defense as soon as we detect a double team situation and attempt to get the ball to the free man. Because this type of defense uses a zone principle, we must now make an adjustment with our offense which we call the "double-up."

DOUBLE-UP

Most teams that employ the double team tactic will usually encourage the guards to advance the ball into the front court. As soon as the offense commits itself, the defense will attempt to close in on the man with the ball while closing off the obvious passing lanes (Diagram 8-8).

As soon as an offensive man realizes that the double team situation is being applied to the ball he calls, "double-up," which initiates the option. When the call is made, 1 immediately looks to pass the ball to the center, 5, who breaks to an open area (Diagram 8-9). We tell 5 that he can go as far as he must, to insure a safe pass. 1 then passes the ball to 5, who immediately turns to pass the ball to the forward on the side away from the pass, in this case 4. 4 should move to the side of the foul lane near the basket if the ball is on the opposite side of the floor. The forward on the same side as the ball, in this case 3, moves toward 1 expecting a pass. When the pass goes to 5, 3 should then cut to the basket, expecting either a pass from 5 or to get the back door rebound position. 5, after passing to either 4 or 3, also goes to the basket to obtain rebound position. 1 and 2 should both remain in the guard positions to be available for release passes from the forwards or the center and also to assume defensive responsibilities.

If the defensive team will not allow a pass to 5 when he breaks high, 1 should then look for the near-side forward. If he is open, 1 should then pass him the ball (Diagram 8-10).

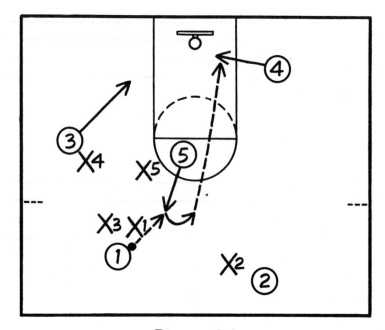

Diagram 8-9

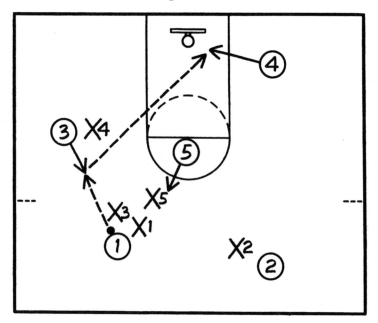

Diagram 8-10

As soon as 3 receives the pass, he should look for 4 under the basket and immediately pass him the ball if he is open.

If 3 decides the pass to 4 is too risky he may then look for 5, who breaks to the foul line toward the ball as 3 catches the pass from 1 (Diagram 8-11). 5 usually is open, as his defensive man, X5, is defending against the pass to 4 under the basket.

If, however, 3 cannot pass the ball to 4 under the basket because the defensive man covering him, X4, has dropped toward the basket, he should then dribble toward the basket himself (Diagram 8-12). If X4 commits himself too early and tries to stop 3, 3 may then pass the ball to 4 for the lay-in. However, if X4 retreats to the basket, 3 may have the high percentage jump shot, with 4 and 5 working for rebound position. 1 and 2 again remain in the guard positions for the release pass and to assume the defensive responsibilities.

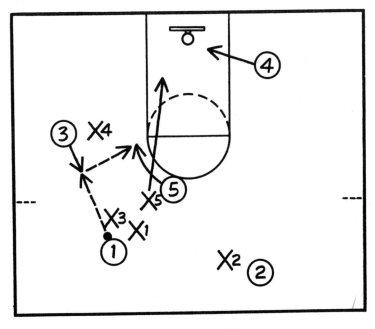

Diagram 8-11

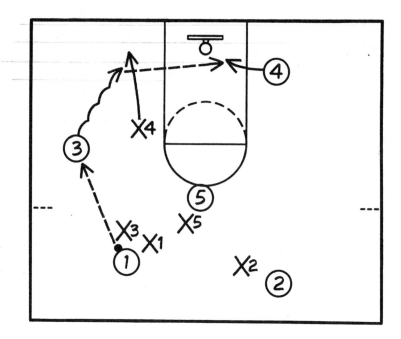

Diagram 8-12

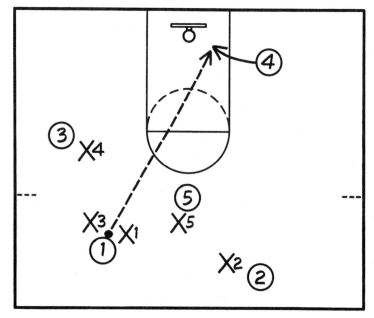

Diagram 8-13

The third option available to 1, if he cannot pass the ball to either 5 or 3, is to look for 4 under the basket (Diagram 8-13). We have found that if all the passing lanes have been overplayed, as in Diagram 8-8, 4 will be open near the basket. We tell 1 to throw a quick high pass that X5 cannot reach. We use the adjectives, "quick" and "high," when describing the pass to our players so that they know we do not mean a lob pass. As the ball goes to 4, 5 and 3 move to the basket to become rebounders and 1 and 2 remain on defense and available for a release pass.

We permit a pass from 1 to 2 only as a last resort when the opponents leave that passing lane open in an attempt to prevent the score (Diagram 8-14). We still attempt to get the ball into the pivot area to 5. If the defensive team allows the pass from 1 to 2 to be made, we usually find that 2 will have the best opportunity to feed the ball to 5.

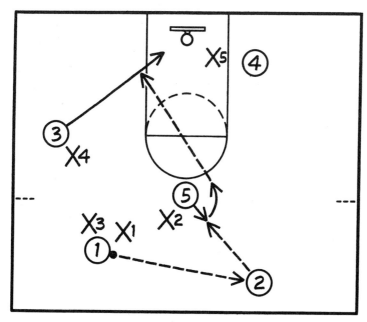

Diagram 8-14

Remember, it is important for your team to be organized against any pressure attack. Not only will this reduce panic but it will instill confidence in your players' ability to defeat pressure defense teams.

HELPFUL HINT IN TEACHING THE TRIDENT

Remember, in the "rotation" option, if 1 should have to pick up his dribble, he may call "help" and 3 can come for a handoff. 1 then cuts to the basket and the option develops as the original Direct Pass Pattern.

9

How the Trident Attacks
Combination Defenses

From time to time most coaches have found the need to use a combination defense against an opponent. We have used combination defenses upon occasion and have found in most cases they have been quite successful. One of the main reasons for this success, we believe, has been the failure of opposing coaches to organize their attack against this type of special defense. In a majority of cases, we have found our opponents have to work out some special maneuvers during a time-out or at the half.

One reason why coaches do not spend time preparing for the various combination defenses is that they do not have to attack them often. As a result they do not figure the preparation time is warranted. We felt it was important to be able to attack these defenses even though we might only have them used against us once or twice a season. Therefore organization against combination defenses seemed necessary because: (1) usually we must win that one game to be a championship contender, and (2) if we lose the game or have considerable difficulty defeating a weaker opponent we will probably be faced with similar defenses, as the scouts will take this information home with them.

The basic principle upon which the combination attack is built is that we try to force a team into a double coverage situation and thus free one or two offensive players completely. We believe that if a team wants to reduce the effectiveness of one or two men in our offense by using multiple coverage, they can do this—unless the offensive players involved are of the "super-star" variety. We then feel that the other players, left pretty much uncovered, will defeat them.

BOX AND ONE

As soon as we realize that the opposition is using a combination defense we call out the type of defense and indicate the player being specially defensed. In this case (Diagram 9-1), we would call "box and one on 2" usually using 2's name. This then is the key for us to go into the combination defense option of the Special Split Pattern by having 1 pass the ball to 5 and scissoring off 5 with 2. As in the regular Special Split Pattern, 3 and 4 then assume the guard positions and the pattern is halted at this point.

We have now forced the defensive team into a double coverage situation on 2 with X2 and X5 both having defensive responsibility for 2 (Diagram 9-2). 5 now becomes a threat to score by turning to face the basket if the defense will permit. If he is open, we want him to shoot from this position. Usually, however, X3 or X1, and sometimes both, will move to prevent the shot. 5 should then pass the ball to the open man, in this case 4. 4 will generally have good jump-shot position; if not, the ball should be moved quickly to either 5 or to 3 who has taken a release position near the top of the foul circle. We have found that we get the high percentage shot before the fourth or fifth pass.

If, when we realize that the opposition is using a combination defense, 1 cannot make the safe pass to 5, he should then pass the ball to 3 and cut diagonally to the opposite side of the foul line, watching for the return pass as he cuts on a give-and-go maneuver. 2 also cuts to the opposite side of the lane from his position looking for the pass (Diagram 9-3). 3, after looking for 1 and 2, should then dribble to an open area near the side of the key to shoot. 4 then takes a release position near the top of the foul circle and the pattern is halted at this point. Again, by making good, sharp passes, 3, 4, or 5 should obtain the good, high percentage jump shot.

In both of these options, 1 and 2 become rebounders and

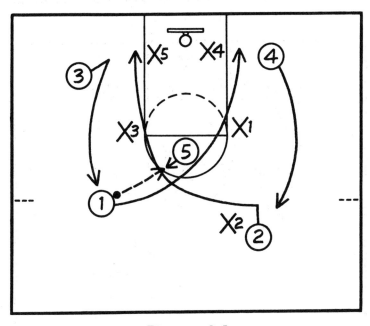

Diagram 9–1

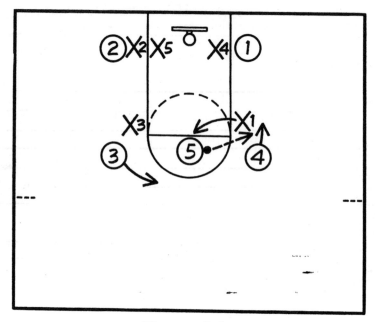

Diagram 9–2

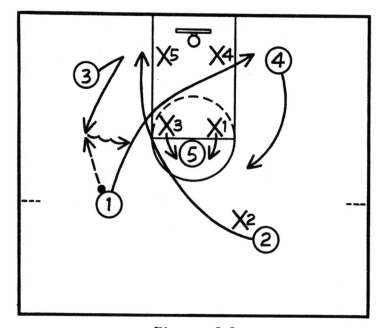

Diagram 9–3

3 and 4 have defensive responsibilities. 5 should also work hard to obtain rebound position and often he can become effective.

TRIANGLE AND TWO

The same two options are used against the Triangle and Two defense. We have found that most teams, when they use this defense, will play our guards man-for-man. This, of course, makes the pattern even more effective (Diagram 9-4). We have now obtained double coverage on both 1 and 2 leaving only X3 to defend against 3, 4, and 5.

Many coaches will also invert their triangle, playing one man deep under the basket and two men near the foul line. (Diagram 9-5). We still use the same options and have three

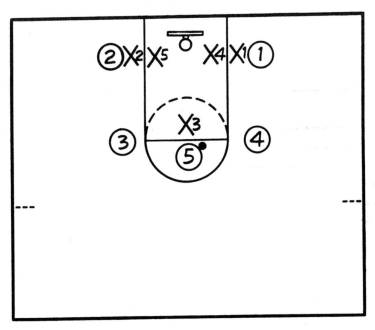

Diagram 9–4

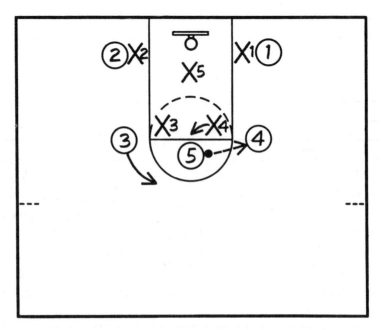

Diagram 9–5

offensive men, 3, 4, and 5, covered by two defensive men, X3 and X4.

In all of the previous situations we stress the importance of 1 and 2 obtaining rebound position. They are told that their major contribution to this particular pattern is to get us the ball for the second and third shot whenever possible. We feel we must take time to explain to our players who are being played man-for-man that they must become strong team players in this situation.

10

Attacking Full-Court Pressure
with the Trident

M any college coaches today are facing
the problems of full-court pressure defenses that
high school coaches faced six to eight years ago.
It has only been in the past few years that college
coaches have had to prepare to meet and beat the
various man-for-man and zone presses.

About six years ago we felt the need to develop a full-court pressure attack since nearly half
of the teams in our conference used full-court
pressure defenses at times other than when trying
to get back in a game in which they were behind.
As a result, we designed an attack that we still
use today.

In designing this full-court press offense we
wanted an attack that would allow us to do the
following things: first, it could be used against any
form of man-for-man or zone press defense; second,
that we not only be able to bring the ball safely

over the ten-second line but that we be able to score from it; third, that the attack be one that we can quickly set up if the opponents should surprise us.

This attack can be used against both man-for-man and zone press defenses. Again, we determine the defense to be either man-for-man or zone, depending upon whether the player controlling the ball is double teamed by the defensive team. A double team situation indicates a form of zone press to us.

ZONE PRESS ATTACK OPTIONS

We always align our men on the floor in the same manner, with the possible exception of the guards, 1 and 2 (Diagram 10-1). Usually we want our poorest dribbling guard to take the ball out-of-bounds. This, however, is not absolutely necessary, particularly when one guard is close to the ball and can get it in play before the defense sets up. We usually make the poorest dribbling guard take the ball out-of-bounds if the defense is already set up.

The guard who takes the ball out-of-bounds, in this case 2, should always stand to either side of the foul lane. 1 should then line up on the opposite side of the foul lane at the junction of the foul lane and foul line. He should be straddling the foul line so that his shoulders are perpendicular to it. 3 is our best ball handling forward and, in most cases, the smaller one. We always play him on the left side of the court at the ten-second line if 4 is right-handed. 4 then takes the other side of the court at the ten-second line. 3 and 4 should straddle the ten-second line facing each other and about 6 feet (two steps) from the sideline. 5 may then line up in the deep post position on either side of the foul lane.

We tell our guards that the defensive team will then play them in one of three ways. First, they will make no attempt to prevent us from making the pass in-bounds (Diagram 10-2). This we call a three-quarter-court press.

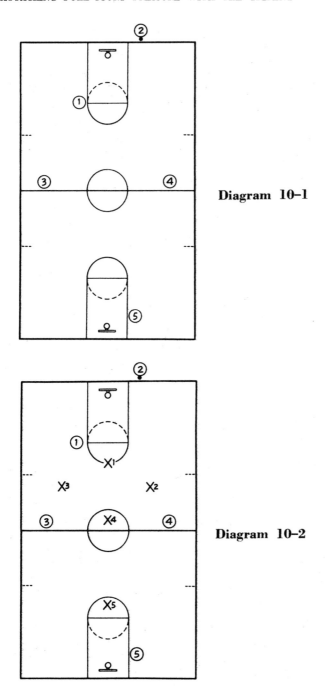

Diagram 10–1

Diagram 10–2

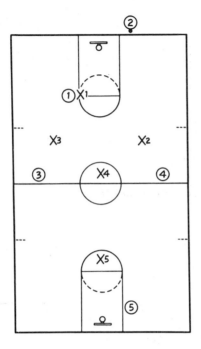

Diagram 10-3

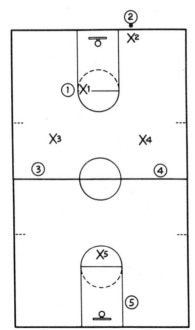

Diagram 10-4

Second, that the opponents will contest the pass-in from the out-of-bounds, with one defensive man on the guard most likely to receive the ball, in this case 1 (Diagram 10-3 or Diagram 10-4). As you can see, they may or may not put a defensive man on the player taking the ball out-of-bounds.

Third, the opponents may defense 1 with two men to prevent the ball from being passed to him (Diagram 10-5).

Since the full-court pressure offense can be used against any type of pressure defense, it is not important for our players to try to determine the type of defense being used. If the defense allows the ball to be passed in to 1, 1 should break toward the ball and receive it as he moves toward 2. As soon as 1 receives the ball, he should look to be sure he is not being double teamed by the defense. If he is not, he should then begin dribbling up the floor, expecting the double team by the defense. As soon as the defense initiates the double team, he should stop his dribble to prepare for the pass (Diagram 10-6). 2, meanwhile, moves in-bounds and to a spot behind and to the opposite side of the floor from 1, expecting a release pass from 1 should he get in trouble.

When 1 begins his dribble he should watch X2 closely. If X2 begins his move too quickly before X4 can cover for him, he may be able to pass directly to 4 (Diagram 10-7). This usually does not happen, but 1 should be alert for the possibility.

As soon as 3 observes X1 and X2 initiating the double team, he breaks into an open area in the middle of the court (Diagram 10-8). 1 then passes the ball to 3 as he breaks free. As soon as 3 receives the ball, he should turn and look for 4 as he breaks across the middle of the court. 3 then passes the ball to 4 and follows his pass. It is good to note here that when 3 receives the ball from 1 he does not dribble but looks immediately for the pass to 4. 3 may find that he will occasionally have to dribble the ball over the ten-second line himself if

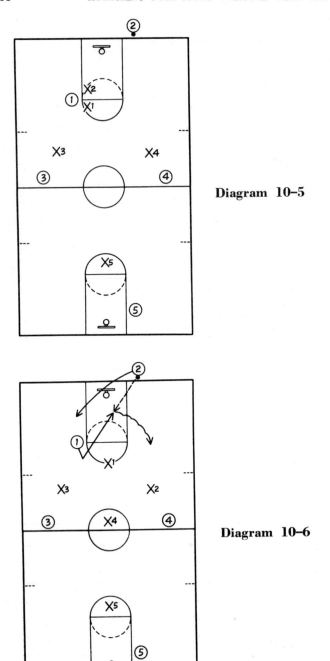

Diagram 10–5

Diagram 10–6

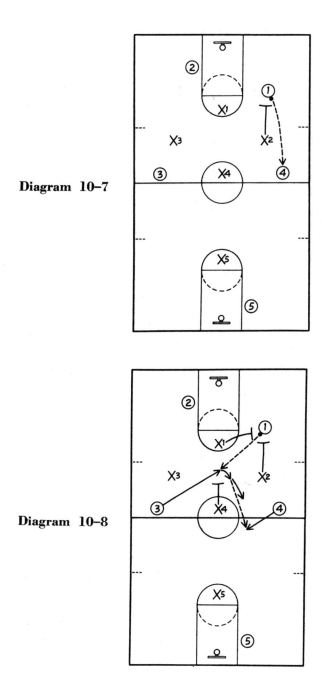

Diagram 10–7

Diagram 10–8

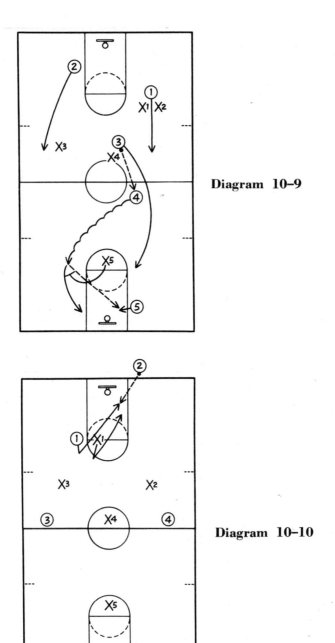

Diagram 10–9

Diagram 10–10

the defense drops off him to cover all the outlet passing lanes.

As 4 receives the ball, he breaks on a fast dribble for the basket. 5, if he is not on the opposite side of the basket from the ball, moves to the back door rebound area. If X5 attempts to stop 4, 4 may then pass the ball to 5 and then move in for the rebound (Diagram 10-9). 3, after passing to 4, then follows his pass and goes to the opposite side of the floor as 4. He should be alert for a release pass and jump shot. If he does not get the ball, however, he then is in position to begin the offense. 1 and 2 take the guard positions and have defensive responsibilities.

If the defense being used by the opponents employs only one man to contest the pass-in from out-of-bounds, we want 1 to fake and cut directly toward the man with the ball, in this case 2 (Diagram 10-10). 2 should then pass the ball to the hip of 1, that is, away from his defensive man, X1.

As soon as 1 receives the ball, he turns and looks for 3 breaking into an open area, usually near the middle of the court. If 3 is open, 1 passes him the ball and the offense is run as before, with 4 breaking across the middle and taking the pass from 3. 4 then takes the ball in on a two-on-one situation, teaming with 5 against X5 (Diagram 10-11).

If, as 1 receives the ball from 2, he is double teamed by X1 and X2 so that he cannot make a safe pass to 3, he may then give the ball to 2 who has assumed a release position (Diagram 10-12). 2 may then pass the ball to 3 if he is open and the offense develops as before.

Should X1, however, play such tough defense that a safe pass may not be made to 1, 3 should break for the ball (Diagram 10-13). 3 usually should give 1 a count or two to free himself for the pass before coming for the ball. It may be noted here that 3 may go anywhere on the floor where he can get open for the pass. The open areas in this case, of course, depend upon the position of the defensive men. Again, when 3 receives

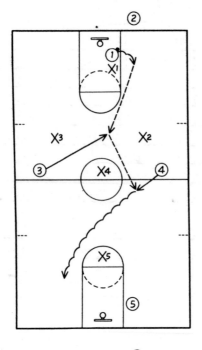

Diagram 10–11

Diagram 10–12

Diagram 10–13

Diagram 10–14

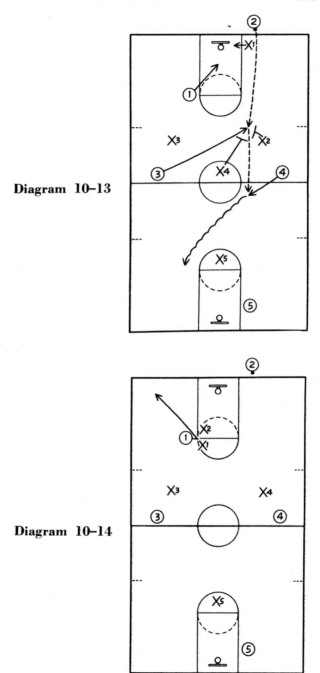

the ball he should look to pass the ball to 4 and continue the offense.

We also allow 3 to come directly for the ball when 1 is being double teamed (Diagram 10-14). In this case, as soon as 1 realizes that the defense has doubled up on him, he cuts to either corner by the base line, clearing the rest of the court for 3.

As soon as 1 clears the area, 3 breaks directly for 2 to receive the ball. When he breaks free, 2 passes him the ball and the offense again develops as before (Diagram 10-15).

It is true, of course, that we do not always get the lay-in or short jumper. We have found, however, that teams which attempt to overplay our offense to prevent the lay-in have seriously curtailed the effectiveness of their press and we have very little difficulty in advancing the ball beyond the ten-second line.

MAN-FOR-MAN ATTACK

As stated before, we use the same alignment against full-court, man-for-man defense as we do against a zone press. Our philosophy, however, is different from the double-team situations, or zone, and the single coverage of the man-for-man. In the man-for-man coverage we attempt to isolate our best dribbler with his defensive man and we feel that he will beat him in the one-on-one situation.

We begin attacking the full-court, man-for-man press by again lining up in the positions indicated earlier in Diagram 10-1. The offense is started in exactly the same way with 1 faking and cutting directly toward the ball (Diagram 10-16). If he is open, 2 should pass him the ball and cut to the opposite side of the court, watching at all times to see if 1 is going to be double teamed. If 1 should be double teamed, we consider the press to be a zone and break it as described

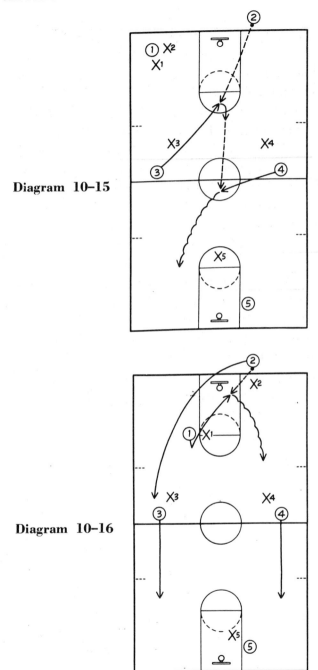

Diagram 10–15

Diagram 10–16

earlier. However, if 1 is not double teamed when he begins dribbling up the court, 2 then continues to the ten-second line to clear the back court for him. 3 and 4, when they see that the defense is using only one-on-one coverage, begin to retreat to their normal forward positions watching for a pass at all times. When 1 brings the ball into the front court, both 3 and 4 should be in position to begin the Trident Offense immediately.

If X1 is such a good defensive man that he forces 1 to stop his dribble, 2 then has the responsibility to help his fellow guard. As 1 stops his dribble, 2 cuts directly toward him to receive the ball. We indicate that 1 should usually throw a bounce pass to 2's hip; that is, away from his defensive man, X2. 1 now follows his pass to get a handoff from 2 (Diagram 10-17).

As 1 crosses the ten-second line, 3 should be available to receive a pass, and we like 1 to initiate the Direct Pass Pattern (Diagram 10-18). We tell 1 that if he is being played aggressively by his defensive man, in this case X2, he can be open on the give-and-go maneuver. 5 should also break into the high post position, expecting the pass from 1 as 1 crosses the ten-second line. If the pass would go to 5, then, of course, the pattern run would be the Special Split.

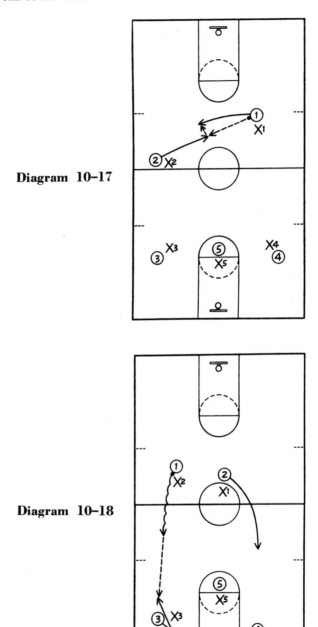

Diagram 10–17

Diagram 10–18

11

Drills to Complement
the Trident Offense

Much of the success enjoyed since the
development of the Trident Offense is attributed
to the drills that are used in practice. These drills
were specifically designed for the Trident Attack;
however, many are so basic that they could be
used for any type of offense. The drills included
in this chapter are the actual drills used every
week to improve the offense.

In deciding the drills that will be used and
the way they will be conducted we have set up
four basic criteria. First, the drill must be simple
to learn and execute. We do not want to spend
a large portion of our practice time teaching drills,
especially early in the season when practice time
is so valuable. This is possibly even more important
to the high school coach than to the college coach,
since a high school team may have its first game
within ten days to two weeks after the first practice session.

177

Second, the objective of the drill must be taught to your players. Most coaches tend to take too much for granted when teaching a new drill and feel that the objective of the drill is so obvious that they need not spend time discussing it. This, however, is leaving too much to chance and is too important to overlook. The players may have a different idea of what the drill is designed for than does the coach, or the players may not even think about why a drill is given but just generally accept the idea that drills are a necessary part of a basket-ball practice session. If the maximum value of a drill is to be achieved, the players must know exactly the purpose for which the drill was designed.

Third, the drill must be intense. By this we mean that players must be completely absorbed in the drill. If the player is not concentrating upon the drill and his responsibility to it, maximum value will not be achieved. The attitude of the coaching staff plays a significant role in the players' performances in drills.

Finally, the drill must relate to your offense. Maximum value or efficiency in terms of results cannot be obtained if the drill does not approximate the type of situations that will occur in the game.

TWO LINE PASSING DRILL

The two line passing drill is the first offensive drill we use during practice. (Diagram 11-1). We feel that for any attack to be successful it must depend upon a strong passing game. This is particularly true of the Trident Offense and as a result considerable time is spent in developing efficient and uniform passing fundamentals. The number of players involved in the drill depends upon the size of the squad and the number of coaches available. We never, however, have more than one drill for each coach so that every pass can be observed by a member of the coaching staff.

We usually attempt to perfect four types of passes with this drill. These are the two-hand push pass, the one-hand bounce pass, the baseball pass, and the two-hand underhand pass.

These are four basic passes that are necessary to the success of the Trident. We also stress the importance of moving to meet the ball in this drill.

The drill is run by having 1 pass the ball to 2, who steps forward to meet the pass. 2 then passes to 3 and the ball continues to move up and back between the two lines.

A variation of the same drill is to have the players follow their pass (Diagram 11-2). 1 passes to 2 and then follows his pass to take 2's position. 2 then passes to 3 and then takes 3's position.

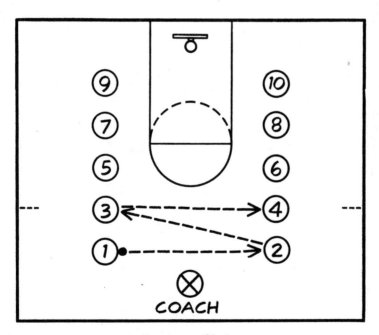

Diagram 11-1

Another variation of this drill that adds considerable ball-handling skill and makes the players concentrate is the double pass and exchange (Diagram 11-3). In this variation 1 passes to 2 and cuts to the side of his next pass which will be to 4. As 1 approaches, 2 hands the ball to 1 and takes 1's place. 1 then hands the ball to 4 who then passes to 3 and begins the double exchange all over again.

HANDOFF DRILL

This is one of the simplest yet most effective drills for improving ball handling on the move and teaching players to meet the ball. As the players become better at handling the ball, you can have them move faster toward each other and prevent them from bouncing the ball. After handing the ball off, the player then moves to the end of the opposite line (Diagram 11-4).

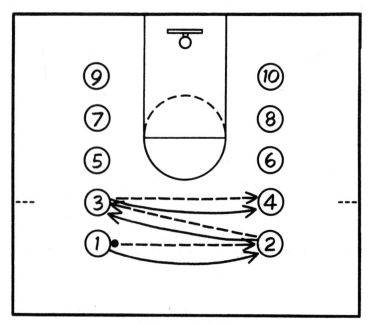

Diagram 11–2

TWO LINE LAY-IN DRILL (Two Basketballs)

We use the two line lay-in drill as a warmup before pro-
ceeding to more vigorous activity. The drill, as we use it, is
run with two basketballs being used and the shooters receiving
the ball so that they need not dribble before making a lay-in.
We want our shooters to run at least half the length of the
gym or more before taking a pass from the rebounder. We have
found that this drill places a premium upon timing, good
passing, and making the lay-ins while going full speed (Diagram 11-5).

GRAPEVINE (Two Basketballs)

The weave or grapevine drill begins with three lines at
center court (Diagram 11-6). In this drill, we again use two

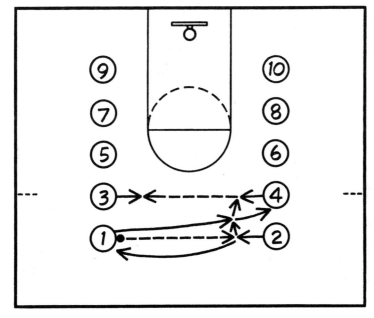

Diagram 11–3

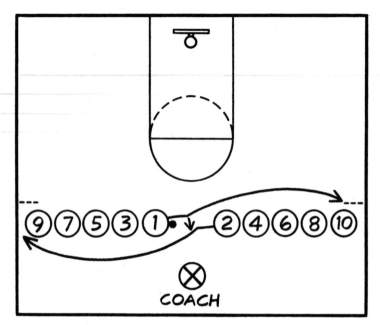

Diagram 11-4

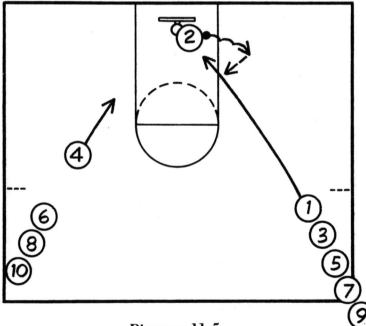

Diagram 11-5

basketballs with the second group of players beginning as the ball is shot by the first group. In this particular drill, we stress the movement of the ball both in moving in for the score and in getting the ball out to the outlet area quickly and safely. This is one of the main drills for emphasizing the speed at which the ball should be moved. We also encourage the man in the middle to work the drill to both sides by having him start the drill on the side opposite the direction from which he received the pass from the outlet area.

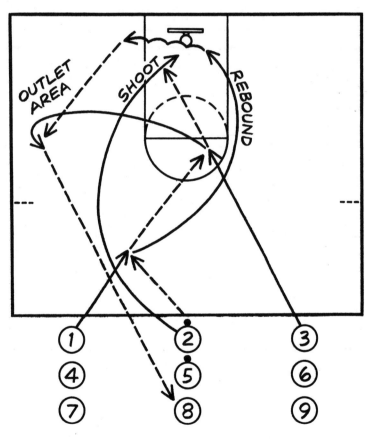

Diagram 11–6

SPOT SHOOTING DRILL

The spot shooting drill is the most important shooting drill
we use. It is so important that we spend some time running
it in every practice session. The drill itself is very simple. We
use it to work on shooting fundamentals, to build confidence,
to work on shooting without taking a dribble, and to work on
following the shot.

In this drill we use four balls and each man rebounds
his own shot. When the shooter gets the ball, he passes it back

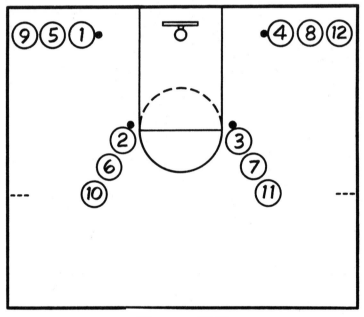

Diagram 11–7

to the next man in line and goes to the next spot to his right. The amount of time we spend with the drill varies from five to 15 or 20 minutes depending upon the abilities of our players (Diagram 11-7).

It is important to use only four spots for practice instead of a larger number because shooting from too many spots reduces the effectiveness of the shooters. If a player has confidence from a few spots on the floor, this will carry over into his shooting even when he is not shooting from a specific area. These also are the areas from which most shots are taken in the Trident Attack.

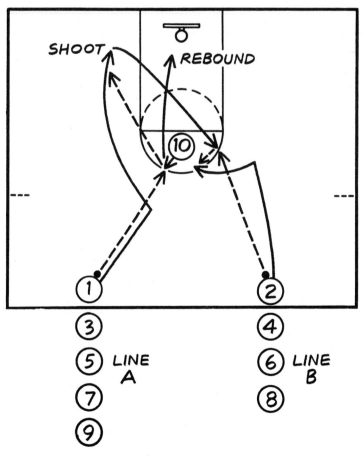

Diagram 11-8

RELEASE PASS JUMP SHOT DRILL

This drill begins with two lines of players at the ten-second line and one player in the high post position (Diagram 11-8). To start, 1 passes the ball to 10 and cuts either to the top of the foul circle or to the side of the foul lane, expecting a release pass from 10 for the shot. Here we stress that 1 makes quick decisive moves, keeps his eyes on the ball, and jumps straight in the air without "drifting" to the side. 10 then rebounds the shot and returns the ball to line A. 10 also goes to the end of line A. 1, after taking the shot, breaks for the high post area and a pass from 2 in line B.

We have found this drill to be quite helpful in teaching the players to get their balance before going straight up on their shot. This greatly improves their accuracy.

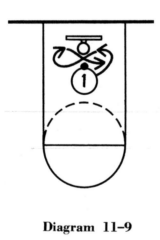

Diagram 11–9

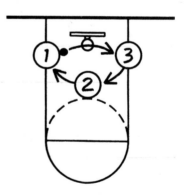

Diagram 11–10

FIGURE 8 HOOK SHOOTING DRILL

The hook shot is one of the best shots in basketball; particularly the driving hook shot. Because of the number of drive-in shots we attempt to get in the Trident Offense, we work with our players to develop a hook shot that is fundamentally sound and in which they can have confidence. We encourage our players to spend at least five minutes each night running the figure 8 hook shooting drill.

This drill begins with 1 standing just in front and facing the basket (Diagram 11-9). The player then steps with his left foot, hooking the ball with his right hand. We insist that the player follow through and face the basket after the shot so he can get his own rebound. He then steps with his right foot and hooks the ball with his left hand. This drill should be run with a rhythm and each shot must be taken alternately between the right and left hands regardless of whether the basket is made or missed.

We feel it is important to stress that the boy be facing the basket upon completion of the shot to insure a good follow through as well as a possible rebound. We also want the ball to go high and soft off the backboard. We tell our players that we would rather have the ball go over the basket than be short since we expect to have the back door rebound position.

TWO HAND TIPPING DRILL

This drill begins with three players 1, 2, and 3, assuming the proper rebounding triangle (Diagram 11-10). 1 has the ball and shoots it over the basket to 3 at the back door rebound position. 3 times his leap to catch the ball at the top of his jump with *both hands* and shoots it back into the basket before landing on the floor. 2 then retrieves the ball and everyone rotates one place clockwise. After a specific period of time, the drill is reversed and rebounds are shot from the other side of the board. We emphasize that the ball, whenever possible, is to be caught with both hands and shot with one on the tip-in. Too many times an easy lay-in rebound is missed because the player uses only one hand instead of two. We also are able, on occasion, to obtain two free throws when an official rules that the rebound was actually a shot.

HOMEWORK DRILL

This drill is run for both the forwards and centers (Diagram 11-11). In this drill, the guards 1 and 2 have the ball in the normal guard positions and 3 and 5 both work their defensive men to be free to receive the ball. The defense may apply as much pressure as they can without fouling the offensive men. This drill continues from one to three minutes without stopping before a new offensive man comes into the drill. (This can also be a fine conditioner early in the season.)

SPEED DRILL (Without Defense) (With Defense)

The speed drill is another basic drill that we use in every practice session. It consists of running the various options of the Trident Offense with all possible speed to improve timing and to commit the options to memory in such a way as to have the players react without actually having to think about what they should do.

After first running the options without a defense we then add defensive players so that the players can operate under more realistic conditions. We work at this drill until the players not only react to the patterns and options of the Trident but also to the defensive situations caused by the defensive men. As a result, we have found that if we can make the offense effective against our own players it becomes even more effec-

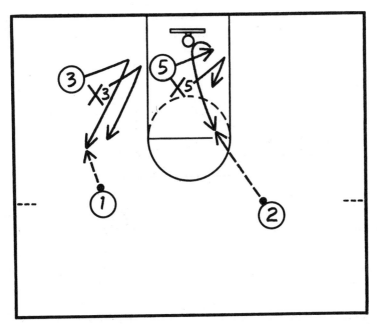

Diagram 11-11

tive against opponents. The patterns we use as speed drills are: Direct Pass Pattern; Bounce Pass Pattern; Special Split; "blind pig"; Check; Double Check; "Regular" zone attack; Overloaded Diamond; Buttonhook; Attacking the Notch, and "rotation."

RUB-OFF DRILL

The rub-off drill is used after the team has become somewhat familiar with the Direct Pass Pattern option of the Trident. We usually work only with the guards and centers in this drill and place particular emphasis upon the center rub-off position and roll to the basket for inside rebound position (Diagram 11-12). We also emphasize the techniques necessary for the offensive guard to control his defensive man and the driving hook shot once he breaks free on the rub-off.

Later we may add a defensive center to the drill and re-

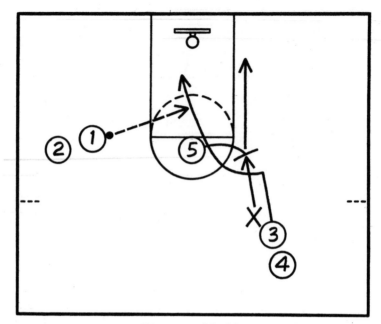

Diagram 11-12

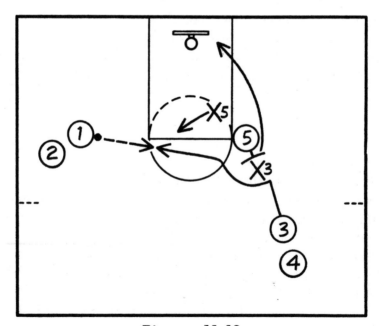

Diagram 11-13

quire the guard to react to a shift. Here we allow the guard to drift to the side of the key for a jump shot (Diagram 11-13).

HIGH-LOW DRILL

The high-low drill is run using only the forwards and centers (Diagram 11-14). Here we emphasize the rub-off maneuver between 5 and 3 and the cut of 3 to the high post area to meet the pass from 1. We also work on the jump shot by 3 and the tip-in by 5 if the defense will permit this. If not, 3 passes the ball to 5 who slides across the foul lane in a high-low maneuver. After passing the ball to 5, 3 then moves quickly to obtain the back door rebound position.

REVERSE DRIVING DRILL

The reverse driving drill again uses only the forwards and centers and is very similar to the high-low drill, except that we stress an additional maneuver. Again 5 drops down the back side of the foul lane so 3 can rub-off his defensive man and break to the high post area for the ball. We again want 3 to look for his jump shot and for 5 on the high-low maneuver. If neither option is available, we want 3 to attempt to beat his man on a drive to the right side, looking for the driving right-hand hook shot (Diagram 11-15). 5, after sliding across the lane, should obtain back door rebound position.

THROW-OUT DRILL (Handoff)

The throw-out drill is used to improve the "throw-out" or reverse option of the Bounce Pass Pattern of the Trident Attack. In this drill we use guards, forwards, and centers. The ball begins in the forward position and is passed to the offside guard, in this case 1, who moves to meet the ball at the top of the foul circle (Diagram 11-16). As soon as 1 receives the ball, 5 breaks up the back side of the foul lane. 1 then bounce passes the ball to 5's outside hip and follows the pass, expecting a handoff from 5 for the drive-in or jump shot. 5 then breaks to the basket for rebound position.

3, after passing to 1, moves to a position to be able to cut quickly off the stationary post. 3 comes off the post just as 5 receives the pass from 1 (Diagram 11-17). 5 then has the option of passing to 3 before 1 cuts by looking for the handoff.

5 always has the option to keep the ball and drive for the basket any time his defensive man, X5, jump-switches to stop 1 (Diagram 11-18). 5 may detect X5's intentions by glancing over his outside shoulder to see if X5 is moving toward 1 as he cuts. If he is, then 5 can pivot on his right foot and drive to the basket.

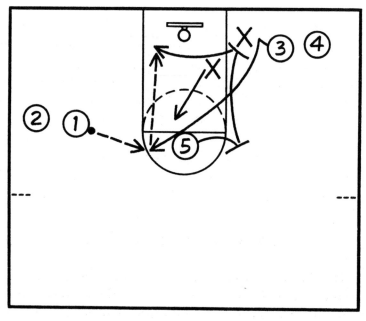

Diagram 11–14

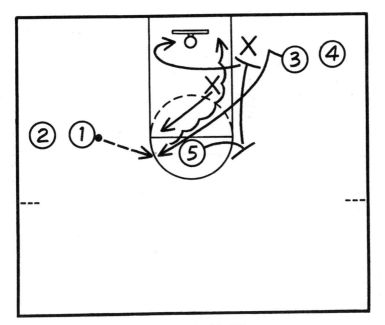

Diagram 11-15

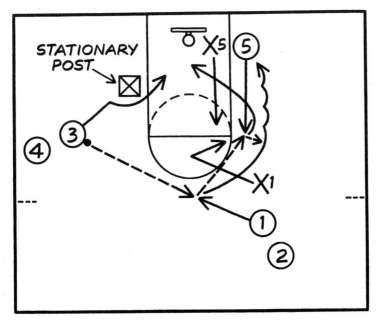

Diagram 11-16

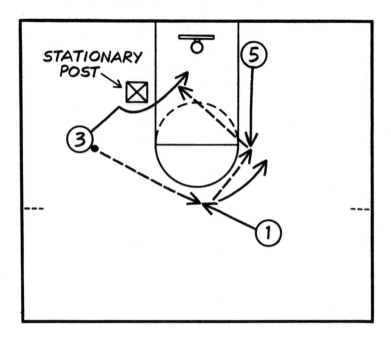

Diagram 11–17

THROW-OUT DRILL (Screen and Roll)

The screen and roll option of the throw-out drill is used when either X1 or X5 overplays the passing lane from 1 to 5 (Diagram 11-19). When this happens, 1 dribbles off a rear pick set by 5 on X1. 1 then attempts to dribble in for the lay-in or good jump shot. If he is stopped by X5, he then attempts to pass to 5 as 5 rolls to the basket.

After both the handoff and pick-and-roll options of the drill have been learned, we then have the defensive men vary their techniques, forcing the offensive players to react to the different defensive situations.

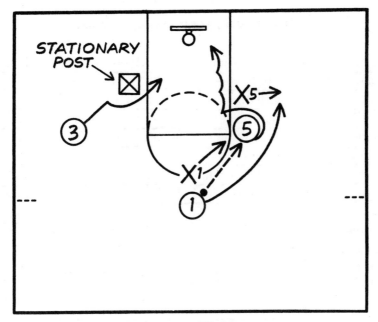

Diagram 11-18

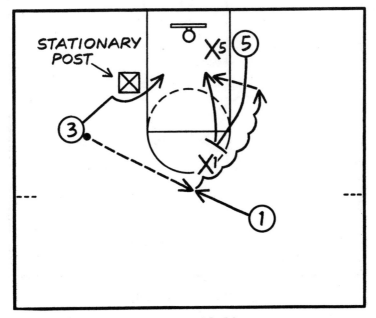

Diagram 11-19

FIVE-MAN CIRCLE PASSING DRILL

This drill is used primarily to work on the two-hand chest pass. We are not only concerned with the fundamentals of this pass, but also with the speed at which it is thrown. In this drill, we want our players to move the ball as quickly and safely as possible as though they were moving the ball in our "Regular" zone attack.

To begin this drill we have our first team space themselves evenly around one of the foul circles, our second team around the center circle, and our third team around the other foul circle. We then ask the players to take two steps backward to increase the distance between them. We then give one player in the circle a basketball, in this case 1 (Diagram 11-20). 1 then makes a quick two-hand chest pass to 3, since we have

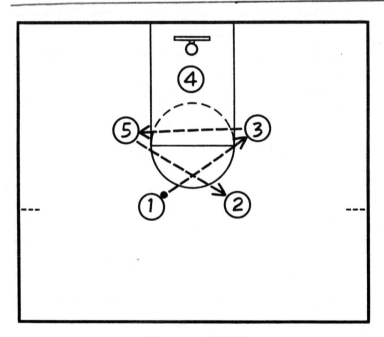

Diagram 11-20

a rule that the passer may not pass to the man adjacent to him. We usually start the drill by passing the ball to the right for a prescribed length of time, then reversing and passing to the left. The players soon learn the maximum speed at which they can safely and accurately move the ball. This is the basic object of this drill.

ZONE PRESS DRILL (Without Defense) (With Defense)

This again is very similar to the speed drill used for the various options of the Trident Offense. We run the zone press drill in every practice session to commit it to memory. This drill consists of running the zone press offense as quickly as possible without a defense so that each player can become familiar with the moves and positions of his teammates.

After the drill is being run properly, we then add a defense to make the situations more realistic and meaningful. We vary the types of pressing defenses used in this drill so that the players will have confidence in their ability to beat any type of pressing defense.

It is important to remember that drills themselves are of little value, but drills properly run to meet specific objectives can be the difference between success and failure.

Index

201